From Stanley Cohn
Christmas, 1983

Fort McHenry

HOME OF THE BRAVE

Front Cover

Top Left:
Looking down the Patapsco River, about 1798

Top Center:
Major George Armistead, in command, 1814

Top Right:
Francis Scott Key watching the battle, 1814

Bottom Left:
World War I medical officers, 1917–18

Bottom Center:
Sketch of Bombardment, September 13, 1814

Bottom Right:
Reunion of the "Old Defenders," Baltimore, 1880

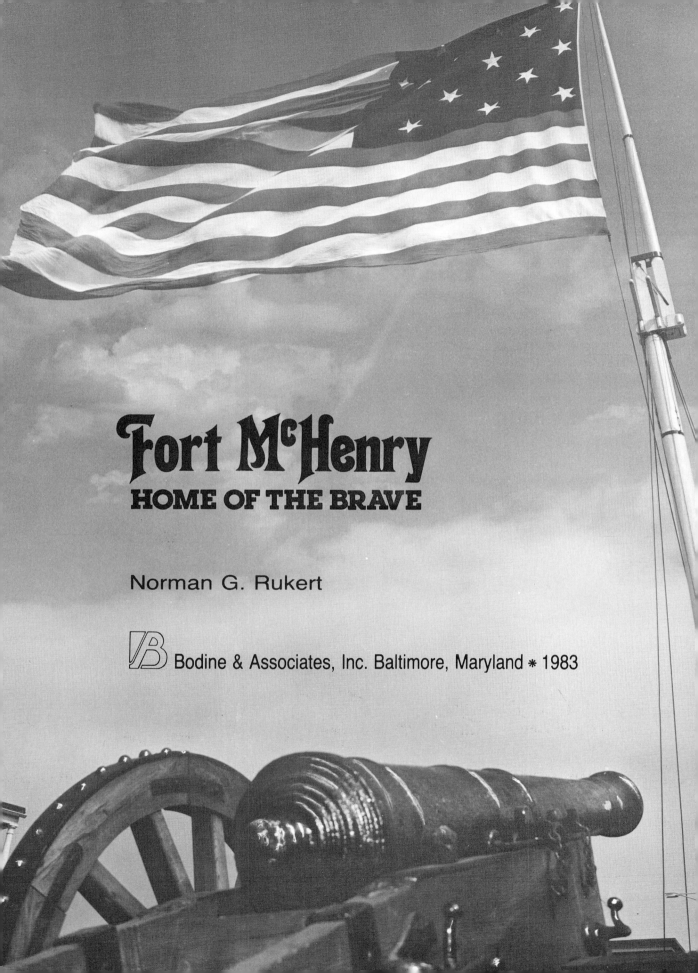

Fort McHenry
HOME OF THE BRAVE

Norman G. Rukert

Bodine & Associates, Inc. Baltimore, Maryland * 1983

Other Books by Norman G. Rukert

The Fells Point Story (1976)
Historic Canton (1978)
Federal Hill (1980)
The Port, Pride of Baltimore (1982)

First Edition

Library of Congress Catalog No. 83-73218
ISBN 910254-24-9
Copyright 1983 by Bodine & Associates, Inc.
Printed in the U.S.A.

Tattoo, Parade Grounds   *A. Aubrey Bodine*

INTRODUCTION

Early one morning in May, 1982, I had an appointment in Canton with a man who usually arrived at work before sunup.

The approach to his office includes many sensations: seagulls, cranes, piers, ships, warehouses, 18-wheel trucks, and potholes. The office is in a building directly across the Inner Harbor from Fort McHenry. In front of the building, Rukert Terminals, is a cannon from the War of 1812 era pointed at the water. I could not then know the significance. Inside Norman Rukert's office I was surrounded by pictures of the port, replicas of ships, citations of merit, and other momentos from a busy life.

Norman had a problem. He had just finished his fourth book and needed another challenge. He was like a computer without a database. As I watched Norman I knew that, for him, the life of the mind was a life of authorship. Norman has written about the port itself, the north shore, lined by Fells Point and Canton, and Federal Hill on the harbor's south side. The site at the end of that peninsula beckoned: Fort McHenry.

Over the months that followed there was the excitement of a new search for information and the quest for historical themes which would interpret this National Historic Shrine around its local, national, and international importance. The result is a book with passages of descriptive color, intrigue, new information, and legend. The book will appeal to young and old, as should a book about Baltimore's most famous fort.

A little known fact about Fort McHenry's "hour of glory" in 1814 is that across the harbor, now the site of Rukert Terminals, cannon also fired on the British fleet. The salvo that shook Britain came from the Fort, but now Norman Rukert has issued a salvo of words and pictures from his headquarters across the harbor. The little cannon in front of Norman's office might remind future Baltimoreans that without the efforts of historians and tellers of tales, the heroic deeds of men and women of yesterday would fade and be forgotten. Norman, in his books about the communities which ring the Inner Harbor, has contributed to the immortality of the people who fought, lived, and worked in our port city on the Chesapeake.

W. Theodore Dürr
Defenders' Day, 1983
University of Baltimore

CONTENTS

ACKNOWLEDGMENTS

As with my previous four histories, the preparation and publication of this volume was made possible by the enthusiasm, interest, and cooperation of many individuals.

I am particularly grateful to Janet Farr who served as my researcher and consultant for this book. She spent countless hours coordinating this project at Fort McHenry and many other institutions, collecting valuable information and illustrations.

Much appreciation is owed Juin A. Crosse, Superintendent, and the National Park Service staff, at Fort McHenry for their help during the researching and writing of this book. Paul Plamann, with his knowledge of the fort's history, provided valuable guidance throughout the project. The resources at Fort McHenry were used extensively, and the cooperation and assistance of the staff—Hyman Schwartzberg, Jerry Backof, Pat Freburger, William Justice, Janet Shirkey, Darschell Washington, and Janet Wiley—was very much appreciated.

I wish to acknowledge the contribution of Scott Sheads, National Park Service, for sharing the results of his extensive research into the fort's history and for his help in locating and photographing illustrative materials at the fort and the National Archives in Washington, D.C. William Stokinger, National Park Service archaeologist, provided much information on the archaeological discoveries of the early history.

Thanks are due those who assisted with the illustrations in this book: Dan Toomey and Eric Davis for their Civil War portraits; Special Consultant John McGarry, U. S. Marine Corps Museum, Washington, D.C., for his research and assistance regarding the uniforms and accouterments of important military periods at the fort; and Marie Mulvenna for her help in gathering illustrative materials.

The staffs of many institutions provided important assistance. I mention particularly: Dr. Morgan Pritchett and the staff of the Maryland Department and Ralph Clayton of the Microform Center of the Enoch Pratt Free Library; The Maryland Historical Society; The Flag House; The Baltimore City Archives; Clem Vitek and the staff of the Baltimore *Sun*; The Maryland Hall of Records, Annapolis; The National Archives, Washington, D.C.

I would like to express my sincere gratitude to James F. Waesche, author of *Baltimore, Annapolis and Chesapeake Country,* for his dedication while editing this book. His valuable suggestions and refinements were much appreciated.

Norman G. Rukert

PROLOGUE

Stay, sentinel of the watch, I pray;
   Bow low thy head in reverence dear;
Tread softly o'er the ramparts gray;
   For Freedom's brow was star-crowned here!
Here Freedom's heavenly hand unfurled
Her starry symbol to the world;
And here we give our vows to thee,
Resplendent Banner of the Free
                        That waves o'er Fort McHenry!

When free men seek for Freedom's Shrine
   In this, our land of liberty,
Then from thy walls her star divine
   Will lead their steps to thee, to thee!
Unheeded never be her calls
While floats her flag above thy walls!
And may thy ramparts ever be
The fortress of the brave and free,
                        O, gallant Fort McHenry!

John F. Gontrum

It was here on this very spot, made sacred by the heroism of the Americans who fought and repulsed the invaders in the War of 1812, that the flag with its 15 broad stripes and 15 bright stars flew on that morning of September 14, 1814, to inspire Francis Scott Key to compose the vibrant verses that became our national anthem.

Yet it was here during the four and a half years of the Civil War that thousands saw the fort as an instrument of military tyranny rather than as a symbol of the "land of the free." It was here that Francis Key Howard was imprisoned on the forty-seventh anniversary of his grandfather's writing of "The Star-Spangled Banner." It was here that George Armistead Appleton, grandson of Colonel George Armistead, the man who commanded Fort McHenry during the British attack in 1814, was also imprisoned.

But it was also here that some 20,000 soldiers wounded in World War I passed for treatment on their way back to duty or to civilian life. Here medical history was made, particularly in plastic and neuro-surgery, as soldiers who had lost portions of their faces left the fort's hospital with new noses, new ears, and other seemingly miraculous manifestations of then-new surgical techniques. It was also here that the country's first school was started to teach veterans telegraphy and typewriting.

But in spite of those milestones, Fort McHenry today is a National Monument and Historic Shrine because of its all-important role in the War of 1812—a war from which Americans emerged with what they had so essentially lacked at its outset: a national character founded on a glory common to all.

BUILDING YEARS . . . 1661–1811

ORT McHenry is located at the tip of a narrow peninsula which juts between the North West and Ferry Branches of Maryland's Patapsco River. The first settler there was Charles Gorsuch, a member of the Society of Friends, who, on February 24, 1661, patented 50 acres and began paying an annual rent of one pound sterling at St. Mary's City, then Maryland's capital. Gorsuch subsequently abandoned the land, so on June 2, 1702, another patent was granted, this one to James Carroll, who first called the area Whetstone.

Although a 1706 Act of the Maryland General Assembly declared Whetstone Point a port of entry, it does not appear that either traders or planters ever availed themselves of its commercial "facilities." But then, on March 29, 1723, iron ore was discovered on the point and the tract was resurveyed. In 1725, Carroll sold it to John Giles for five pounds of sterling. Two years later, Giles made something of a profit by selling all the iron ore "open and discovered or shut and not yet discovered" to the Principio Company for 300 pounds sterling and 20 pounds current money of Maryland.

The Principio Company, established in England in the early 1700s, was an association of British iron-masters, merchants, and capitalists. Their purpose was to smelt ore from the Chesapeake Bay area to supply themselves and to sell as pig- and bar-iron in England. The company's furnace was near Perryville, at the head of the Chesapeake Bay. That site had been chosen for several reasons: iron ore was close at hand, there was a creek with a waterfall to provide power for the bellows and hammer, and a dense growth of timber offered an ample source of charcoal. Furthermore, the proximity of the Bay assured an abundance of oyster shells for lime. After 1727, however, most of the company's iron ore was being transported by water from the Whetstone Point mines.

At the outbreak of the Revolutionary War, Whetstone Point acquired strategic as well as economic value. Since at that time all of Baltimore's port facilities were on the North West Branch of the Patapsco, the Point could not be overlooked in any plan to erect defenses to guard the water approaches to the city. When, in the spring of 1776, the British sloop *Otter* sailed up Chesapeake Bay, the citizens of Baltimore became so alarmed that, under the direction of the Maryland Council of Safety, they immediately began to build fortifications on Whetstone Point. An 18-gun battery was planned by James Alcock, construction began, and Captain Nathaniel Smith accepted the command of the battery.

Three massive chains, supported by floating blocks of wood, were stretched across the river to Lazaretto Point, leaving open a narrow passage for vessels on the side next to the battery, directly under the guns. The channel was further obstructed by a line of 22 sunken schooners.

Workers then labored at constructing the water battery, which soon evolved into both an upper and a lower battery. By the middle of March the word "fort" also began appearing in correspondence received by the Council. On March 16, for example, a letter announced: "Our Fort at Whetstone is ready to mount 8 guns, and we shall use every exertion to expedite it." However, that July, another letter indicated that the "fortification" was still incomplete. By the end of the year, plans for a magazine at Whetstone Point were well advanced, but this structure may not have been built. As the Revolution progressed, these fortifications were still being strengthened, and a shot-furnace was erected near the batteries. During time of battle, cannon balls could be loaded into the shot-furnace and heated to a cherry-red. They would then be loaded into the cannon with a forked instrument and fired. On impact they would explode and, it was hoped, set fire to the wooden ships.

During the Revolution, the Principio Furnace turned out 18 cannon and hundreds of cannon balls for Fort Whetstone. In answer to that tangible contribution to the Colonies' war effort, the British burned the plant down, but Thomas Russell, the ironmaster, eluded His Majesty's troops and returned to rebuild the furnaces in time to make more cannon and munitions for the Continental Army.

In 1780 an act was passed by the General Assembly "to seize, confiscate and appropriate, all British property within this State." The following year the property of the Principio Company on Whetstone Point, containing 400 acres, was sold in lots to a number of prominent Baltimoreans.

Because the British never threatened Baltimore after 1776—at least not during the Revolution—Fort Whetstone was gradually abandoned. The deterioration of the boom caused it to be taken up in the fall of 1778. By January 29, 1780, the garrison at the fort had been reduced from five to two soldiers. An order was issued on July 19, 1780, to sell everything at the fort except the cannon and the furniture. That

Francis Guy's View of Baltimore Harbor (1800), Fort McHenry in center right   *Maryland Historical Society*

fall, all but four cannon, many of which had decayed carriages, were ordered removed.

No detailed description of the fort or its water batteries has been found. A 1781 map of the Point shows a true star fort without bastions (projections from a fortification), an upper and a lower water battery of 27 embrasures (openings in a wall having sides which slant outward), a flagstaff, and four buildings outside the star fort. A 1792 map shows a similar fort with but a single battery and no outbuildings. It is probable that the star fort and the batteries were of simple earthen construction with perhaps some timber reinforcements.

Until 1793 the fortifications on Whetstone Point remained exclusively under the control of the state of Maryland. In that year, however, war between France and

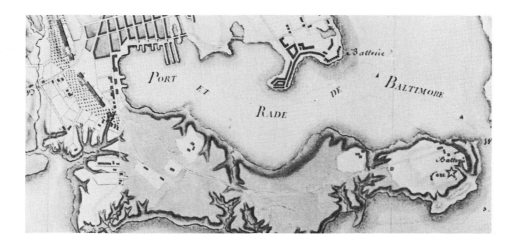

1792 Map of Fort Whetstone   *Library of Congress*

Great Britain convinced state leaders that it would be advisable to place the Point at the disposal of the federal government. That transaction was accomplished in the following, somewhat condescending, resolution passed by the Legislature in 1793:

"Whereas, the United States may think it necessary to erect a fort, arsenal, or other military works or building on Whetstone Point for public defense; therefore, Resolved, that upon the application of the President of the United States to the Governor for permission to erect a fort, arsenal, or other military works on the said Point for the purpose aforesaid, the Governor shall and may grant the same."

In the spring of 1794, Congress passed legislation authorizing erection of fortifications along the Atlantic Coast. A report submitted to Congress recommended the modest expenditure of $4,225 for the fortifications of Baltimore:

Baltimore, Twenty-eight Pieces	
Parapets, embrasures, and platforms	
for batteries, for 28 piece	*$2,015.44*
A redoubt, with four embrasures	*810.00*
Two magazines	*400.00*
Block-house or barracks	*500.00*
Contingencies	*500.00*
	$4,225.44

The federal government now accepted the offer from Maryland. Secretary of War Henry Knox wrote Governor Thomas Sim Lee that he had appointed Major John Jacob Ulrich Rivardi to plan the fortifications for both Baltimore and Alexandria, Virginia. Major Rivardi was one of several French engineers and artillery officers who had immigrated to America after the French Revolution. Since the United States did not yet have a military academy for training engineers, the French officers played an important role in this country's first system of fortifications.

Rivardi's instructions held him to the figure of $4,225.44. His specific orders concerning construction called for the simplest of fortifications: earthen walls, plank embrasures, and timber magazines. All told, the garrison was intended to consist of one officer and 30 enlisted men. Before beginning the work, Rivardi was to obtain the approval of the governor of Maryland.

By mid-April Rivardi had prepared his plans, employed a superintendent of construction, and overseen the beginning of work on a lower water battery. Upon arrival in Baltimore, he had inspected the remains of the 1776 fortifications. He had found the lower battery in bad repair and the upper one of poor design. Furthermore, someone had dug a huge pit in the area to obtain iron ore or red ocher. Rivardi had decided to rebuild the two batteries according to his own design: the lower battery would contain 20 guns rather than its former 11; the upper unit would have about eight pieces.

More pertinent is Rivardi's evaluation of the 1776 star fort itself:

"The star fort never was entirely finished, and the greater part of the ditch is filled up with the earth of the breastworks; that kind of redoubt, always bad in itself, (the fires being oblique, and the salient as well as the entrant angles indefensible) is rendered still more so, the perpendicular of construction being one-fourth, instead of one-third of the side of the polygone."

The implication is strong that the first fort had consisted of earthworks only, and that no masonry had been employed. Rivardi planned to construct two small bastions in order to flank most of "the entrant and salient angles." In one of the bastions he planned to construct an underground magazine, the gun "platform itself service as a bomb proof." Apparently he did not plan to use brick in the walls of the ramparts: "I shall want 1,280 feet solid timber, for the facing of some part of the works, at one shilling a foot; 1,400 palisades to freize and palisade the berm and ditch of those two sides of the redoubts which are not flanked by the bastions, besides the necessary timber for the facing the embrasures and covering the platforms." Rivardi drew plans of the proposed work, forwarding one set to the Secretary of War. These plans have not yet been discovered.

A week later, he further informed the Secretary that he was constructing a frame barracks of 40 by 16 feet. Eighteen workmen were already on the job, and he had requisitioned 100 shovels, 30 pickaxes, 36 pickets, 70 wheelbarrows, two gins with block and falls, 25,000 bricks, and one crowbar.

Samuel Dodge, a civilian who was sometimes referred to as a lieutenant, became the superintendent of construction at Fort Whetstone, and Rivardi hurried on to Alexandria to plan its works. On May 19, 1794, Dodge reported that the lower battery was "nearly to its heights" and that he had begun sodding it. He added: "Some part of the upper work is considerably forward and if the citizens continue to give the assistance [slave labor] they have expect the chief of the work will be raised and finished in about sixty days."

During the summer of 1794, Dodge made several reports to Secretary Knox. While he discussed the batteries at length, he made very little reference to the fort itself. On one occasion he mentioned purchasing timber and plank for "the bridge." Whether he was referring to the bridge across the ditch to the gate of the fort is unknown. By the end of the summer, he acknowledged sadly that all the work was far behind owing to much sickness among the workmen.

Despite Rivardi's and Dodge's best efforts, the work at Whetstone Point failed to reach anything nearing completion. In July of the following year, although not much improvement had been seen in the speed of construction, the federal government did see fit to spend $3,200 for seven and a half acres adjoining Fort Whetstone.

Finally, in January, 1796, Congress learned that a battery and a barracks had been completed and that some guns had been mounted at the fort. Still, 1796 and 1797 witnessed relatively little additional construction. In February, 1797, Congressman Samuel Smith criticized the plans for the fortification. He complained that Rivardi (without mentioning him by name) had conceived too grandiose a plan for the fort. The congressman pointed out that ships over 36 guns could not enter Baltimore's harbor because of its shallow channel. He complained, too, that no magazine had been built: "When the commander of the fort arrived there, he found 27 barrels of powder lying above his barrack. The cattle had also free intercourse with the barracks, nor was there any defense against them."

World events were quickly coming to Smith's aid. Congress, alarmed at the deteriorating relations with France in 1798, voted for much more than repair funds. It made $250,000 available for coastal defense, and Secretary of War James McHenry dispatched yet another French engineer, Major Louis Tousard, to Baltimore to review the works at Whetstone Point and to furnish "a plan and estimate if such additions hereto may be considered absolutely indispensible to the protection of the City."

Major Tousard surveyed the existing defense works and submitted recommendations for their improvement. He regarded as insufficient the $20,000 which had been allotted for the purpose, and, rather than risk his professional reputation, he turned his plans over to a committee of prominent Baltimoreans who agreed to raise

James McHenry

National Park Service, Fort McHenry

an additional $10,963.44 by popular subscription and to supervise the program. The committee was successful in raising the money, and Major Tousard was able to complete the improvements by the summer of 1799. The committee's hope of reimbursement by the Maryland Legislature or the federal government does not appear to have been realized.

In the fall of 1799, a third French engineer, Jean Foncin, arrived in Baltimore. He disagreed with the plans of both Rivardi and Tousard. While his criticism of plans already approved by both the state and federal governments caused some embarrassment, Foncin succeeded in persuading all concerned that his concepts were best.

Although it is not known exactly the ways in which Foncin's ideas differed, the five-bastioned, pentagonal structure which is Fort McHenry today reflects his plans. Secretary of War James McHenry once wrote of him:

> *"I have employed on the Fortifications erecting at Baltimore, in the capacity of Engineer, a French Gentleman of the name of Foncin, and that evidence of ability in his profession by correcting errors of much consequence, in the original plan of the works, as well as of assiduity in Superintending and directing their progress, induced me to raise the compensation he was first engaged at. This Gentleman I would recommend to be continued in employ as heretofore."*

Carrying out Foncin's plans, the Army spent $12,000 in 1799, $53,000 in 1800, and $8,185 in 1801. Included in the money spent in 1800 was a $5,000 item for an

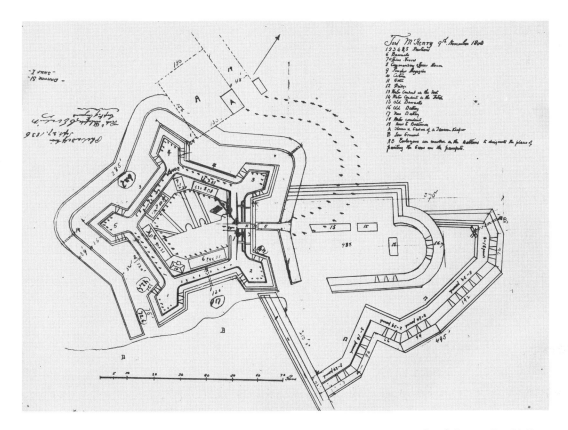

Map of 1803—Earliest known plan of the Fort

National Park Service, Fort McHenry

additional eleven and three-quarters acres. In 1801, a Mr. Steele became the superintendent of construction; soldiers from the garrison performed much of the labor. The works were probably essentially finished by 1802, for the Army spent barely $1,000 that year. Based on the available evidence, it can be assumed that completed by 1802 were: the masonry and earthen, five-bastioned, pentagonal fort; the two brick barracks; the two brick structures containing officers' quarters; and a magazine.

A detachment of troops was stationed at the fort at least as early as 1797 under the command of Captain Staats Morris. The earliest description of the garrison yet found, dated June 20, 1802 (a few days after Morris left the Army), showed one company of artillery stationed there.

Around the turn of the century, James McHenry, Secretary of War and a resident of Baltimore, was honored when his name was bestowed on the fort. As Secretary of War he had been instrumental in the final plans and completion of the fort on Whetstone Point.

McHenry had been born in Ballymena, County Antrim, Ireland, on November 6, 1753, the son of Daniel and Agnes McHenry. He received a classical education in Dublin, but because of poor health, he sailed to America and settled in Philadelphia in 1771. In that city he met Margaret Allison Caldwell and married her on January 8, 1784.

McHenry studied medicine under Dr. Benjamin Rush. Subsequently, having joined the Continental Army in 1776, he accompanied George Washington to the camp at Cambridge. He was the senior surgeon at Valley Forge in 1778. Later that year he became Washington's secretary. In 1780 he was transferred to the staff of the Marquis de Lafayette and remained with him until the end of the war.

He held many high offices in Maryland and, in 1787, became the state's delegate to the Constitutional Convention, where he labored to secure the ratification of the Constitution. He was also a member of the Continental Congress from 1791 to 1796, at which time he was made Secretary of War in Washington's cabinet. He held that office through Washington's administration and, subsequently, under President John Adams until 1801.

In private life, McHenry published a Baltimore directory in 1807. In 1813 he served as the second president of a Bible Society founded in Baltimore in 1810. He died on May 3, 1816, and was buried in Baltimore's Westminster Churchyard.

The earliest known plan of the fort named for James McHenry is dated November 9, 1803. The cartographer did not sign his name, but it has been suggested that since the scale shown is a French measure, this map may be a copy of Foncin's plan. On it, each flank of each of the five bastions has two gun embrasures; the fronts of the bastions have none. A well-defined ditch surrounds the fort on four sides; on the fifth side, which faces east, the ground is indicated as being low. A row of trees is shown planted around the parade ground; another row is on the terreplein (the horizontal platform behind a parapet where the guns are mounted). Each of the bastions had six trees planted symetrically. The purpose of the trees seems to have been to help bind together the earthen ramparts.

Although the fort was still new, the barracks required more than $300 in repairs in 1803. That same year the quartermaster asked for permission to purchase a flag locally. He informed the military agent (forerunner of the quartermaster) in Philadelphia that the sailmakers in Baltimore wanted $67 for a flag.

For the next years, until the outbreak of the War in 1812, Fort McHenry witnessed routine maintenance and some minor construction. Captain George Peter's 1808 organization of the first mobile horse-drawn artillery unit in the United States

Army was the most interesting event to occur at the fort during this period. The carriages and limbers (the detachable front parts of the gun carriages, usually supporting an ammunition chest) for the two six-pound pieces were constructed by the garrison's own artificers.

In 1811, Secretary of War William Eustis described Fort McHenry as being "a regular pentagon of masonry, calculated for thirty guns, a water battery, with ten heavy guns mounted, a brick magazine that will contain three hundred barrels of powder, with brick barracks for two companies of men and officers; without the fort, a wooden barrack for one company, also a brick store and gun house."

1811 . . .

It was a year when dark clouds of war were gathering. If the storm broke over Baltimore, would the fort on Whetstone Point—so long abuilding—be strong enough to defend the city?

First horse-drawn artillery unit makes its appearance at Fort McHenry

Company of Military Historians

Revolutionary War

Fort Whetstone, later renamed Fort McHenry Defense of Baltimore—1776–1783

The fear of a British attack forced the citizens of Baltimore to begin work on the city's defense. A Committee of Safety chose Whetstone Point for construction of an earthen fort.

Fort Whetstone was manned by local militia, groups of citizen soldiers who volunteered for duty. They wore a variety of uniforms and carried a mixture of weapons.

Some wore the black cocked hat, worn at an angle so the musket wouldn't knock it off. Others wore knit caps embroidered with patriotic mottos.

It is not known when the first American flag was raised at Fort Whetstone. Whatever day it was, it is certain the volunteer soldiers cheered "huzza" as it flew in the harbor breezes.

The hunting shirt was a long coat of linen with fringe attached to shed the rain. Some officers had tailors create fashionable military uniforms. Most men however, came to the fort in their everyday work clothes.

THE WAR CLOUDS GATHER
1793–1812

The INTERNATIONAL DRAMA in which the star fort on the Patapsco was to play so important a role had its opening acts staged in Europe. In 1793, England had entered the war against France. For the remainder of the 18th century, and into the early years of the 19th, the two super-powers of their era engaged in a life-or-death struggle.

As it became clear that neither could win a purely military victory, each began to wage economic as well as armed warfare, proclaiming blockades and other trade-restricting measures. The United States, which at that time possessed the largest and most active neutral trading fleet on the seas, found those tactics especially noisome.

Although the policies of both powers were irritating to the young republic, Britain's gradually became more onerous than Napoleon's because the unchallenged superiority of the former's navy enabled her to enforce her blockades tightly. Then too, the *manner* in which these blockades and restrictions were executed exasperated the United States. For some years Britain had intimidated American ships. Then, in 1807, she had issued a series of Orders in Council which forbade Americans to trade with European countries. Not only had the English blockaded the French coast, they also started seizing American vessels they suspected of trading with their continental enemy.

Furthermore, British ships patrolled America's coastline and subjected United States vessels to harassment even in their own territorial waters. Once seized, the ships were tried by foreign admiralty courts. Naturally the practice evoked great bitterness among Americans.

Anti-British sentiments were also aroused by the practice of impressment. Because of the meager pay, harsh discipline, and brutal living conditions of life on the British ships, there was widespread desertion among their sailors. Therefore, in order to meet their required quota of sailors, the British claimed that they had the right to stop American vessels and remove suspected deserters and former subjects, even those who had legally acquired American citizenship. Although the Americans had continually protested those actions, they continued unabated.

For two decades, this country tried to use diplomacy to secure recognition of its neutral rights. It enacted embargoes and nonintercourse acts, but nothing was successful. America's lack of military strength and the split in public opinion regarding the wisdom of declaring war against England continued to delay armed hostilities.

Admiral Cockburn Burning and Plundering Havre de Grace

Maryland Historical Society

Although the East was reluctant to go to war because the loss of an occasional ship or sailor was a small price to pay for the profits being made by the banking and shipping circles, the West and South, where strong anti-British sentiments prevailed, harbored no such restraint. There was a strong expansionist feeling among the land-hungry settlers and talk of occupying Canada and acquiring Florida, then a province of Spain, England's ally. The West and South were experiencing trouble with the Indians as well as a depression and a decrease in the fur trade. In the minds of many Americans, England was directly responsible for their difficulties.

Finally, in June of 1812, President James Madison was compelled to act. He sent his "war message" to Congress, citing the wrongs which England had committed against the United States and noting the insults hurled at the honor of America. First the House and then the Senate responded to his proposal. That same month, America's "Second War of Independence" was formally declared.

The vote in favor of war was close, however, and it showed that the people were not strongly united behind the declaration. New England was almost solidly opposed. Federalists joined in Congress to vote against the war, and, in the Senate, the vote was a slim majority of 19 in favor and 13 opposed.

The United States was not prepared in 1812 for a military confrontation with the British. The American Navy, in comparison to the mighty and seemingly invincible Royal Navy, consisted of a few ships. It seemed as though there would not be enough arms and equipment for war, and the Army, lacking in leadership and military training, was disorganized.

Walter Lord, in *The Dawn's Early Light,* has written: "Economically, America seemed almost hopelessly weak. Committed to low taxes, the administration tried to finance the war by borrowing, but money proved hard to get. Foreign banks were leery, while New England, the wealthiest section of the country, declined to cooperate. Soon Washington was practically broke—Congress felt it couldn't even afford $6,000 to pay the salaries of two assistant Secretaries of War."

However, the war began as fighting broke out on the Canadian border. Regular troops were sent there, and the Maryland Militia was called into service to garrison Fort McHenry. Within four months after Madison's war declaration, Baltimore merchants sent to sea 42 privateers equipped with 330 guns and from 2,800 to 3,000 sailors. These sleek Baltimore clippers became thorns in the sides of the English Navy, harassing them in every sector of the globe—even in their home ports.

In March, 1813, England sent out a squadron of ten warships, under the command of Admiral George Cockburn, and declared America's Atlantic coastline (except for the New England states) to be in a state of blockade. British ships entered the Chesapeake Bay and began a campaign of devastation, plundering, and destruction on both shores. Raiding parties burned Frenchtown and Havre de Grace and cruised up the Potomac to within 50 miles of Washington itself.

As alarm spread through Baltimore, the adequacy of Fort McHenry's defenses was questioned. But local authorities were not idle, and on March 11, 1813, Governor Levin Winder visited Baltimore and directed Major General Samuel Smith, Commander of the 3rd Division of Maryland Militia, the main body of troops in the area, to "take the earliest opportunity of making the necessary arrangements for the defense of the port of Baltimore."

Admiral George Cockburn, British Naval Commander   *Brenton's Naval History*

Vice Admiral Alexander Cochrane, Commander of the Naval Expedition against Baltimore   *Brenton's Naval History*

On March 13, Sam Smith wrote to Secretary of War John Armstrong about the defenses of Baltimore: "The vicinity of the enemy and his means of rapid movement has caused an apprehension for the safety of this important city." And, he said, he was ready "to present a force of militia every way prepared of at least 2,000 men."

Smith was a strong, aggressive figure with a personal history of service to his country and its people. He was born in Carlisle, Pennsylvania, on July 27, 1752, the son of John and Mary Smith. The Smith family moved to Baltimore in 1760, and John soon became one of the wealthiest merchants in the city. Samuel, after two years at an academy in Elkton, Maryland, entered his father's counting house. The year was 1767, and Samuel was all of 15 years of age!

In 1775, the precocious Smith organized a company of volunteers and entered the Revolution against England. He fought in the battle of Long Island, covered the rear of the American Army in its retreat across New Jersey, and was with Washington at Valley Forge and the Battle of Monmouth. As commander of Fort Mifflin, near Philadelphia, he held out for some 40 days, helping keep Howe's fleet at bay and thus contributing to Burgoyne's surrender at Saratoga, which marked the turning point of the war.

Later in the war, he served as Colonel of the Militia in Baltimore. In 1783, he was appointed the city's port warden, and in 1793, he was elected to represent a Baltimore district in Congress. He was re-elected to that body repeatedly during the ensuing ten years. His services in the lower house of Congress ended in 1803, when he was elected to the United States Senate. He served in the Senate until 1814.

Major General Robert Ross, Commander of the British Land Forces in the Chesapeake Region

National Park Service, Fort McHenry

General Samuel Smith, Commander of Baltimore's Defenses   *Peale Museum*

On March 18, 1813, pursuant to Governor Winder's orders, Smith inspected Fort McHenry and again reported to John Armstrong, Secretary of War:

"I have this instant returned from Fort McHenry. There is much to be done there. The gate is of pine and might be knocked down by a few strokes of an axe. The outer works consist of two open batteries; one nearly on a level with the water it is faced with brick and has space for thirty guns. It has not one, nor has it any platforms and yet it is the most important work against ships attempting an attack or to pass. The other is immediately above this and its guns fire over the lower work. It is here that ten guns, without carriages, are mounted in full preparation for action. I agree with Major Lloyd Beall, the Fort's commander, that if attacked it would be essential for twenty more guns, especially for the lower battery. The fort is in good order and the men, guns and platforms are clean, neat and in military condition. The fort's strength of 52 regulars is insufficient and it is absolutely necessary that at least one hundred and fifty regular Artillerists be ordered to the Fort."

In April, in answer to increasing concern about the British intentions, the Mayor and City Council of Baltimore created a special governmental agency to be known as the Committee of Public Supply. Staffed by the mayor and other important citizens, the Committee's job was to take all steps necessary for the city's defense. Smith suggested that the Committee assume the duty of provisioning the militia, hoping that the city could be reimbursed by the federal government for its expenditures.

Made up of leading citizens, businessmen, and bankers, the Committee soon became the most important agency concerned with Baltimore's defense because it could tap the physical and financial resources of the city as no other group could. Beginning with only $20,000, the Committee soon acquired more than $500,000 in loans from city banks. The Committee acted immediately and decisively to provide needed materials and men instead of relying on often slow and hesitant state or federal aid. It sought Smith's recommendations and never failed to carry them out.

April also saw more work at Fort McHenry. Before the close of the month, Major Beall had received specific orders from Washington to platform each bastion at a height sufficient to allow the cannon to be fixed *en barbette,* i.e., directly over the parapet. He was instructed to employ as many militia and as many citizens as could "work to advantage." Secretary Armstrong was prepared to fund the effort. General Smith was unsure of Beall's ability to accomplish the task and wrote to Armstrong: "Major Beall is not an Engineer, nor have I much knowledge of fortifications. We want an Engineer to be on the spot."

That engineer appeared in the person of Colonel Decius Wadsworth, who visited the fort and criticized the plans for improving it. In his report, he urged that the gate be given better protection by constructing an earthen embankment outside the main ditch of the fort. Furthermore, he suggested that a covered trench or passage should lead from the gateway to the batteries so as to provide safe communication between them. He also noted that "the heavy guns within the Fort should have been placed on the faces of the bastions and not on the flanks which should have been reserved for the field pieces and infantry."

In early May of 1813, General Smith wrote a discouraging letter to the Secretary of War. He said that Colonel Wadsworth had "discharged one half the labours. The work of course progresses, as if we were in a profound peace." Furthermore, as stated, Major Beall was not cooperating as fully as he might. Beall was insisting that his company of 52 regulars, *and* their families, have full run of the fort and its barracks. Smith, on the other hand, thought that at least 350 men, mostly infantry, should be

Major George Armistead (as brevet lieutenant colonel), Commander of the brave defenders of Fort McHenry

Peale Museum

in the fort every night, and he finally wrote Beall's superior urging him to remove all wives from the fort. "Every available room should be used to cover the Soldiers of the Garrison from the weather," he wrote, and "the stationing within the fort [of] as many Artillerists as are necessary for the Guns and of the Infantry to repel an Assault. The assigning Quarters for the Officers should be barely sufficient for comfort not for ease."

Throughout the spring of 1813, Smith marched the militia to Fort McHenry twice a week for training, "the Artillery at the Guns and the Infantry at the Curtains in the Fort." Major Beall cooperated in the training but continued to resist the housing of the militia within the fort. Perhaps because of this conflict of opinion, Beall left Fort McHenry in the summer of 1813.

The very able young Major George Armistead replaced him as commander. George Armistead had been born at New Market, Virginia, on April 10, 1780. He entered the United States Army as Second Lieutenant in 1799; he was appointed assistant military agent at Fort Niagara in 1802 and assistant paymaster in 1806. In October of 1810, he married Louisa Hughes, of Baltimore, sister of Christopher Hughes, *chargé d'affaires* in Denmark, Norway, and Sweden. He rose to the rank of major of the 3rd Artillery in 1813 and distinguished himself at the capture of Fort George in Canada, in May of that year.

Major Armistead was concerned about the lack of a flag at the fort and wrote to General Sam Smith in June:

> "We, Sir, are ready at Fort McHenry to defend Baltimore against invading by the enemy. That is to say, we are ready except that we have no suitable ensign to display over the Star Fort, and it is my desire to have a flag so large that the British will have no difficulty in seeing it from a distance."

Walter Lord has written that Armistead "soon got his wish. Sometime that summer a committee of three high-ranking officers—General John Stricker, of the city's 5th Regiment, Commodore Joshua Barney, commander of a small fleet of gunboats and barges, and Colonel William McDonald, of the Maryland 6th Regiment—called on Mary Young Pickersgill, a widow who normally specialized in making house flags for Baltimore's far-flung merchant ships. The men explained their needs, and Mrs. Pickersgill accepted the order."

With the assistance of her 13-year-old daughter, Caroline, she spent the next several weeks cutting and measuring the stars and stripes. Four hundred yards of "First Quality" long-fibered English wool bunting were required for the making of the flag. (It is ironic that British fabric had to be used, but the desired material was not manufactured in America at that time.)

Since the task of piecing together the huge flag's 15 stars, eight red stripes, and seven white stripes required more space than even the big upstairs bedroom of the Pickersgill house could provide, Mary arranged to use the malthouse of a local brewery.

When finished, the flag measured 42 by 30 feet. Each star was 26 inches from point to point, each stripe 24 inches wide. Started in July, it was delivered by the Pickersgills to Major Armistead at Fort McHenry on August 19. Its cost was $405.90. During the same time, Mrs. Pickersgill also made a smaller "storm flag" for the fort; it measured only 17 by 25 feet and cost only $168.54.

During the fall of 1813 and the spring of 1814, some minor construction was completed at the fort. The invasion scare of 1813 had spotlighted the serious absence of a source of fresh water there. For years a daily detail of soldiers had taken a rowboat to a city well and filled casks for the garrison. Engineers had made several attempts to sink a well, but the water had consistently proved unfit to drink. The Army's quartermaster in Baltimore, Major Paul Bentalou, approached the superintendent of the city's waterworks, John Davis, in search of a solution. Davis believed that he could dig a productive well, and he and the army reached agreement on a contract.

After a number of unsuccessful borings, Davis finally hit pure water which flowed at a regular rate of 18 gallons a minute. The entire well was bricked, and according to a contemporary observer, "a more perfect cylinder or tube could not be easily conceived." A major engineering feat, Davis's 95-foot-deep well served the fort for many years.

As preparations for the defense of Baltimore continued at the star fort, the government in Washington continued to receive discouraging news from abroad. On June 13, Albert Gallatin, an American peace negotiator, wrote from London of possible British intentions: "To use their own language they mean to inflict on America a chastisement that will teach her that war is not to be declared against Great Britain with impunity." Furthermore, Gallatin continued, ". . . I think it probable Washington and New York are the places the capture of which would most gratify the enemy and Norfolk, Baltimore and the collected manufacturing establishments of the Brandywine and Rhode Island are also in danger."

Gallatin's suppositions were to prove remarkably accurate, for, in the summer of 1814, the enemy's fleet in the Bay was augmented and placed under the command of Vice Admiral Alexander Cochrane. In addition, the capitulation of Napoleon at Waterloo permitted the War Office to transfer four battle-hardened regiments from the continent to cooperate with the fleet that had been harassing the Chesapeake region. Admiral Cockburn took this opportunity to advise the army commander, Major General Robert Ross, of the defenseless state of the city of Washington, and urged

Receipt for the Flag from Mary Pickersgill   *The Flag House*

The Burning of Washington on August 24, 1814 (unknown artist)   *Library of Congress*

him to take advantage of the situation.

On August 19, Ross disembarked his forces at Benedict, on the Patuxent River, and on the next day moved his troops slowly toward Washington. In the meantime, a naval party under Cockburn ascended the river and compelled the Americans to burn the remnants of a flotilla of small gunboats that had been under the command of Commodore Joshua Barney. At Upper Marlboro, Ross was joined by Cockburn's naval detachment, and on August 24, the combined force resumed its march toward the capital.

At Bladensburg, the British encountered an army of raw militia hastily collected for the defense of Washington by Brigadier General William Winder, nephew of the Governor of Maryland. The Battle of Bladensburg represents America's military low point during the War of 1812. The inexperienced troops, confused by unclear orders and demoralized by inept leadership, were easily swept aside by the experienced British regiments. That evening the enemy entered Washington unopposed. After a brief period of occupation, during which the Federal buildings were destroyed, Ross moved his troops back to their transports.

Ross and Cochrane remained off the Patuxent for several days, awaiting the return of warships which had been detached on special missions. The most successful of those was the feat of one Captain Gordon, who had led several vessels up the Potomac, collected what amounted to a ransom from the city of Alexandria, and returned safely despite frequent American efforts to intercept his small squadron.

When all the scattered units had returned, Cochrane ordered the vessels to set sail, and the fleet moved northward up the Bay towards Baltimore, their next objective.

Baltimore, a larger, wealthier, and more commercially important city than Washington, was, accordingly, a more desirable military objective than the capital. In the bustling port city the British could confiscate the contents of loaded warehouses, seize three American warships nearing completion in the harbor, and destroy shipyards which were outfitting privateers. Aside from those purely military considerations, Cochrane and Ross were not averse to punishing a city which was a hotbed of anti-British sentiment—and a city from whose harbor had sailed many of the privateers which were successfully raiding British commerce.

Baltimore, however, was not defenseless and had been preparing, under the leadership of Smith, for the anticipated attack. A Committee of Vigilance and Safety had been formed on August 24 (the day of the Bladensburg attack) to replace the Committee of Public Supply. Records show that the new Committee was even stronger and more efficient than its predecessor. It had complete responsibility for defending the city, administering it during the time of crisis, maintaining law and order, raising money to purchase supplies, and providing medical care for the soldiers and aid to the needy. This Committee was also charged with guarding against defeatist attitudes among the citizenry. Most importantly, it mobilized all citizens not subject to military service to work on the defenses. All members of the Committee were elected by the citizens rather than appointed by the mayor as had been the case with the Committee of Public Safety. However, they were still from the merchant-business class and therefore had access to the groups which controlled Baltimore's wealth. The new Committee of Vigilance and Safety became as loyal to Smith as its antecedent had been.

According to Lord, as the details of the disasters at Bladensburg and Washington rolled in on August 25, "Brigadier General John Stricker, commanding Baltimore's own militia brigade, stalked into the Council Chamber where the Committee of Vigilance and Safety was meeting. With him came three other men: Commodore Perry, in town to take over the new frigate *Java;* Captain Robert T. Spence, another senior naval officer, and Major George Armistead."

Together they called for all-out resistance. Burying the usual inter-service rivalries, they also urged that a single over-all commander be appointed for the city's defenses. The man they wanted was General Smith. The Committee agreed and appointed a delegation led by Colonel John Eager Howard, a prominent Baltimorean and Revolutionary War hero, to call on the General. Smith accepted, subject to one condition: he wanted Govenor Levin Winder's sanction, including whatever extended powers might be necessary to do the job.

An emissary was sent to Annapolis. The next day, he was back with the Governor's blessing. It proved a masterpiece of evasion, for apart from relationship considerations, Levin Winder was faced with another most delicate problem. Normally, Brigadier General William Winder, Commanding General of the 10th Military District and a regular, outranked Smith, a militia officer. But if called into federal service, Smith, a major general, would outrank Winder, a brigadier. The hitch was that nobody had called Smith into federal service. Under the presidential order of the preceding July, General Winder had the authority to do so, but he had never exercised it. On the other hand, Governor Winder had no power in such matters at all. The Governor solved the problem by simply *implying* that Smith had been called into federal service. He sent this message back to General Smith:

> "By the requisition of the President of the United States of the 4th of July last, one Major General is required of this state. In conformity to which, you have been selected."

To defend Baltimore, Smith had at his disposal a force of 15,000, consisting of Maryland, Pennsylvania, and Virginia militia, a few regular army units, and about 1,000 sailors under Commodore John Rodgers. Reports of the conduct of the untrained militia at Bladensburg had not escaped Smith's attention, and he decided to wage a strong defensive action.

As a final precautionary step, Smith approached the merchants of Baltimore and proposed that they sink their ships in the channel between the fort and Lazaretto Point. These ships would provide a barrier to the invading British warships. Since the enemy was rapidly approaching the Patapsco, the merchants acquiesced and, one by one, their ships were sunk. They settled upon the bottom of the channel, and they waited. Also waiting were the defenders of Fort McHenry.

THE ENEMY IS UPON US!

THE TENSION in Baltimore was palpable. The enemy was at hand, but where would he strike? And when?

The answer came quickly, on September 11, 1814, when blasts from warning cannon on Court House Green shattered the Sunday morning calm. Cries of alarm swept through the streets like wildfire. "The enemy is upon us! Every man to his appointed station!"

Twelve miles from the city, at the mouth of the Patapsco off North Point, lay 50 ships flying British colors. To the now-beseiged Baltimoreans, the Union Jacks might as well have been skulls and crossbones.

Among the 50 ships were ten transports carrying some 6,000 troops—not just any troops, but members of Wellington's "Invincibles" and veterans of Nelson's campaigns, the very men who had brought down the mighty Napoleon. Now, victorious after August's rout at Bladensburg, emboldened by their easy sack of Washington, they were eager to make equally short work of their next target.

In Baltimore, General Sam Smith lay in wait. With him were some 15,000 men, largely Baltimore militiamen, who were protected by the mile-long arc of earthworks which had been thrown up around the eastern approaches to the city. As his headquarters site, Smith had selected Hampstead Hill (now part of Patterson Park), a high ridge which commanded a sweeping view of the harbor and the road leading in from North Point.

Having anticipated the enemy's plan, General Smith dispatched General John Stricker and 1,700 men from Hampstead Hill. Their orders: harass the British as they advanced toward the city and delay them as long as possible. That very Sunday afternoon, Stricker and his men marched out Philadelphia Road to Long-Log Lane (today's North Point Boulevard). That night they made camp in a defensive formation, with their right flank along the banks of Bear Creek and their left near Bread and Cheese Creek.

Before the first light of dawn on Monday morning, the British were up and about. Boat after boat began to carry soldiers from their transports to the shore. In command of the invaders was General Robert Ross, who had served with distinction in Holland, Egypt, and France. With him rode the ranking naval officer, Rear Admiral George Cockburn, the man who had directed the pillaging of Chesapeake Bay ports and plantations for the past year.

When they had proceeded about four miles up Patapsco Neck, Ross, Cockburn, and six other officers stopped at the house of a local farmer, Robert Gorsuch, and ordered him to fix breakfast for them. As the reluctant host served each dish, he was forced to taste the food. Finally, when his "guests" had eaten their fill, Gorsuch mustered the courage to ask them if they would return for supper. The reply came from Ross.

"No," the general snapped arrogantly, "I shall eat my supper in Baltimore or in Hell!"

No sooner had the words left his mouth when the firing of muskets was heard in the distance. Galloping to the scene, the officers found the advance guards of their own forces engaged with a small party of Americans. Just then, a shot came from nearby. It struck General Ross with such impact that he fell from his horse.

Hastily, Admiral Cockburn and his fellow officers lifted the wounded commander and took cover in a nearby woods.

A messenger was sent to bring a horse and cart. When that crude vehicle arrived, the stricken officer, resting on blankets, was taken from the field. He never made it back to the fleet. Commending his wife and family to the protection of the government he had served so well, General Ross died within sight of the farmhouse where he had so contemptuously announced his plans for supper.

Death of General Ross at Battle of North Point

Library of Congress

According to local tradition, Ross was killed by two young Baltimore sharp-shooters, Daniel Wells and Henry C. McComas. No one will ever know for certain, because the two teenagers were themselves killed in the skirmish. Today they lie buried in a vault in Aisquith Square. Over the vault is a monument erected in the young men's honor on September 12, 1858..

After the death of General Ross, in the words of historians Harold I. Lessem and George C. Mackenzie, "The command of the British forces devolved upon Colonel Arthur Brooke who, in the opinion of a fellow officer, was 'better calculated to lead a battalion, than to guide an army.' Resuming their advance, the British army soon encountered the main body of Stricker's brigade drawn up along a line which Stricker had skillfully selected.

"Brooke's tactics were designed to envelope both flanks of the American line, with the heaviest pressure being exerted initially on Stricker's left. As soon as he became aware of Brooke's intention, Stricker moved two regiments and additional artillery to the threatened sector. His plan to wage a determined defensive action was completely upset, however, when his unit on the extreme left, the Fifty-First regiment, 'delivered one random fire and retreated precipitately . . .'

"Although the panic spread to a few companies, the balance of the American force stood fast in the face of the approaching enemy until Stricker ordered them to fall back on the regiment which he held in reserve. The brigade retired in good order, and in compliance with arrangments previously made with Smith, Stricker posted his brigade on the left, half a mile in advance of the main defense lines of Baltimore."

The whole engagement had lasted just 55 minutes, but it had been hotly fought. The American casualties were 35 killed and 115 wounded or missing. The British loss was estimated at twice those numbers. In contrast to the strategy they had followed after Bladensburg, the invaders did not attempt to take advantage of their success; instead, they bivouacked on the field. As for Stricker's men, they had been driven back, but they had not been demoralized—and they had accomplished their mission, which had been to fight a delaying action.

By this time, Colonel Brooke had been fully impressed with the existence of systematic fortifications, too formidable to attack without the cooperation of the fleet.

To render effective assistance to Brooke's army, it was necessary for Admiral Cochrane to reduce Fort McHenry, which guarded the entrance to Baltimore harbor. At last the fort, which had stood unchallenged for 38 years, was to be called to duty. The foe it faced was formidable indeed, for Cochrane's fleet consisted in part of:

A. War Ships
Tonnant, *80 guns (Flagship of the fleet during most of the campaign)*
Albion, *74 guns*
Royal Oak, *74 guns*
Ramillies, *74 guns*
Asia, *74 guns*
Diadem, *64 guns*
Severn, *50 guns (Flagship of Rear Admiral George Cockburn)*
Melpomene, *38 guns*
Surprize, *38 guns (Flagship of Admiral George Cochrane during the bombardment, due to its shallower draft)*
Trave, *36–38 guns*
Hebrus, *36–38 guns*
Euraylus, *36 guns*

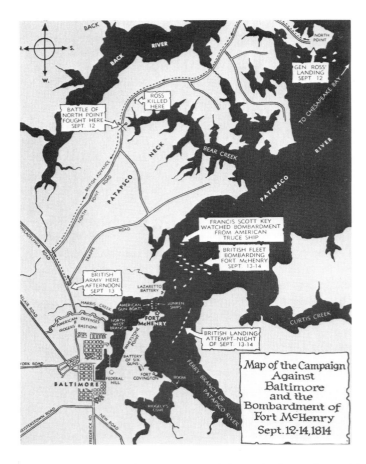

Campaign Map—The British forces in the Chesapeake Region and the Bombardment of Fort McHenry   *Frederic Ray*

Havannuh, *36 guns*
Menelaus, *36 guns*
Seahorse, *16 guns*
Fairy, *12 guns*
Madagascar, *(unknown)*

B. Bomb Ships
Meteor, *18 guns*
Volcano, *16 guns*
Terror, *10 guns*
Aetna, *8 guns*
Devastation, *8 guns*

C. Rocket Ship
Erebus, *18 guns*

D. Schooner
Cockchafer, *(unknown)*

Early in the morning of September 13, 16 warships, including five bomb ships and the *Erebus,* equipped with rocket launchers, dropped anchor about two miles below Fort McHenry.

At Fort McHenry, Major Armistead studied the ominous arc of British ships lying just out of his range. He alerted all the units (about 1,000 men) under his command, which included:

U.S. Corps of Artillery	Commanded by Captain Frederick Evans
Baltimore Fencibles	Captain Joseph H. Nicholson
Washington Artillerists	Captain John Berry
Baltimore Independent Artillery	Captain Charles Pennington
U.S. Sea Fencibles (Two companies)	Captain Matthew S. Bunbury and Captain William H. Addison
Detachment of U.S. Flotilla (Chesapeake Flotilla)	Sailing Master Samuel Rodman
Detachments of the 12th, 14th, 36th and 38th U.S. Infantry	Lieutenant Colonel William Stewart and Major Samuel Lane

Regular artillerists under Captain Evans and volunteers under Captain Nicholson manned the bastions in the star fort. The commands of Bunbury, Addison, Rodman, Berry, and Pennington were stationed in the lower works. The infantry, under Stewart and Lane, were placed in the outer ditch, to meet the British if they tried to land.

With the expected arrival of British forces at hand, Commodore John Rodgers issued a warning to the other harbor defenses manned principally by sailors under his command. These defenses consisted of:

Lazaretto Battery

Lazaretto lies directly across the North West Branch of the Patapsco River from Fort McHenry. (The word Lazaretto means "fever hospital" in Italian.) In 1801,

Map of 1814

National Park Service, Fort McHenry

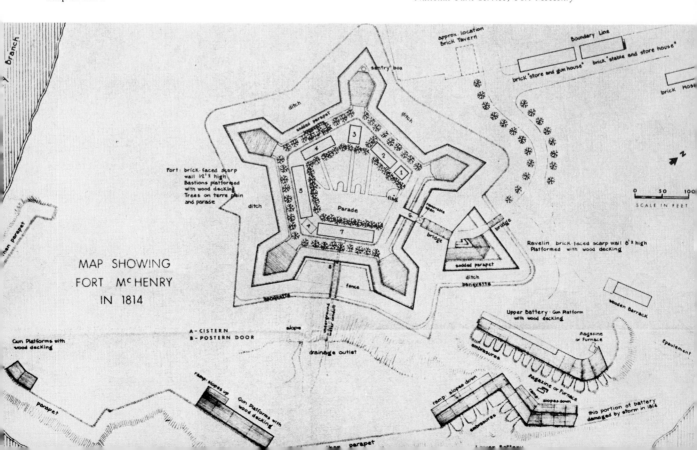

MAP SHOWING FORT McHENRY IN 1814

A - CISTERN
B - POSTERN DOOR

the Maryland Assembly had passed an act to erect a hospital for people afflicted with dreaded contagious diseases. The resulting building was of brick and was three and a half stories high. During August, 1814, a battery of three 18-pounders, mounted on traveling carriages, had been placed there under the command of Lieutenant Solomon Rutter, of the Chesapeake Flotilla. Another lieutenant of the same corps, Solomon Frazier, was in command of gunboats which were moored behind the sunken vessels in the passage between the Lazaretto and Fort McHenry.

Battery Babcock

Located one and a quarter miles west of Fort McHenry on the Ferry Branch of the Patapsco River and named after Captain Samuel Babcock, the U.S. Engineer who had constructed it in the spring of 1813, this battery was described as a fort of an "uncomplicated nature . . . An earthen breastwork, four feet high, was the battery's main feature. Although a magazine was ordered for it, a hole in the hill sixty feet in back of the guns served that purpose." The battery mounted six French 18-pounders. Prior to the battle, it was manned by members of Captain George Stiles's Marine Artillerists. On September 12, Sailing Master John A. Webster, of Joshua Barney's Chesapeake Flotilla, took command. With him were 52 flotillamen.

Fort Wood

Also known as the "circular battery" because of its design, Fort Wood was located about 600 yards behind Battery Babcock. Its primary function was to serve as a rear defense redoubt. The fort had a magazine located in the center of its circular battery. Mounted on naval carriages were seven 24-pounders under the command of Lieutenant George Budd, U.S. Navy. The number of seamen serving under him is unknown, but because of the weight of each cannon, at least 12 men would have been needed to serve each gun.

Fort Covington

Fort Covington was also situated along the shores of the Ferry Branch, about a quarter of a mile west of Battery Babcock. The fort stood on two and three-quarters acres of ground and was armed with a battery of seven French guns. Enclosed by a brick wall, it had a magazine and quarters for a company of men. Prior to the battle, a corps of U.S. Sea Fencibles under the command of Captain William Addison had been stationed there. On September 12, 1814, the Sea Fencibles, sick with fever, were replaced with a detachment of 80 seamen under the command of Lieutenant Henry Newcomb of the U.S. Frigate *Guerriere*.

Fells Point and Federal Hill

At Fells Point there were three naval vessels: the U.S. Frigate *Java,* still without her masts, and the U.S. Navy's Sloops of War *Erie* and *Ontario*. Only the *Erie* had her guns mounted and was ready for action. A battery, consisting of one six-pounder, was mounted on Federal Hill under the command of Sailing Master Leonard Hall of the *Ontario*.

To guard against a surprise blow, Lieutenant Rutter at Lazaretto and Major Armistead quickly worked out a set of challenges for the night. The password would be "William," the answer, "Eutaw."

As Walter Lord writes, "Armistead himself was worn to the bone. Professionally, there was the loneliness of command—he and apparently he alone knew that Fort McHenry's magazine was not bombproof. Personally, there was a great concern for his wife, Louisa. He had sent her off to safety at Gettysburg, but she was expecting a baby and he continued to worry."

THE BOMBARDMENT

AT 5:00 A.M., as the British bomb vessels weighed anchor and began edging toward Fort McHenry, heavy torrents of rain swept across the area. This rain would continue to pour throughout the night. By 6:30, the British fired a couple of shots to check the range, but found they weren't close enough. At 7:00, the bomb vessels opened with heavy fire directed toward the fort from a distance of two miles. They kept up this steady bombardment until 3:00 that afternoon.

Major Armistead, the late 19th century historian Benson Lossing says, "immediately opened the batteries of Fort McHenry upon them and kept up a brisk fire for some time from his guns and mortars, when, to his great chagrin, he found that his missiles fell short and were harmless. The garrison was exposed to a tremendous shower of shells for several hours without power to inflict injury in turn, or even to check the fury of the assault; yet they kept at their posts, and endured the trial with cool courage and great fortitude."

About 2:00 P.M., British shells landed directly on the southwest bastion and exploded with a blinding flash. For a brief second, everything was lost amid the fire and smoke. When the air cleared, the defenders could see that a 24-pounder had been dismounted. Its crew lay sprawled around it. Two young defenders of the fort, Lieutenant Levi Claggett and Sergeant John Clemm, lay dead; several others were injured.

A short time later, a shell crashed through the roof of the magazine. Miraculously, it did not go off, and, as it lay there sputtering, an unrecorded hero doused its fuse. Still, the hit was too close a call for Major Armistead. He ordered the powder barrels cleared out of the magazine and scattered under the rear walls of the fort. It was better to risk one or two soldiers than see the whole fort go up.

The confusion in the fort produced by these incidents was observed by Admiral Cochrane, who, hoping to profit by it, ordered three of his bomb-vessels to move closer in order to increase their effectiveness.

Writes Lossing, "This movement delighted Armistead. His turn for inflicting injury had come and he quickly took advantage of it. He ordered a general cannonade and bombardment from every part of the fort; and so severe was his punishment of the venturesome intruders, that within half an hour they fell back to their old anchorage. The rocket-vessel *Erebus* was so much injured they were compelled to send a division of small boats to tow her beyond the range of Armistead's guns to save her from destruction. The garrison gave three cheers and the firing ceased."

Admiral Cochrane quickly changed plans. Obviously, the fort had not been

Bombs Bursting in Air (circa 1816)

subdued after all. Signal flags were run up aboard the *Surprize,* and the squadrons pulled back out of range. The British, however, once they regained their former positions of safety, began a second bombardment which was even more furious and steady than the first.

That evening, Admiral Cochrane decided to stage a diversionary attack on Ferry Branch. He hoped it would confuse the Americans and draw some of the troops who were facing the British at Hampstead Hill. To lead the attack he selected Captain Charles Napier, skipper of the frigate *Euryalus.*

His plan was to take a force of seamen and marines, aboard small boats, into Ferry Branch, west of Fort McHenry. After covering a mile and a half they would anchor and wait until 1:00 A.M. At that hour the fleet would start to bombard Fort McHenry and so would Napier. It was important to put on a good show, for the attack upon Hampstead Hill would be made promptly at 2:00 A.M.

Shortly after 9:00 P.M., the fire from the British ships quieted, then ceased altogether. The British hope was that the Americans would take this cessation as the end of the day's bombardment.

At midnight, the operation began. Some 1,200 picked men were sent from the fleet in barges. They were equipped with scaling ladders and other implements for storming the fort. The rain and darkness immediately had their effect, for the last 11 barges became separated from their mates, missed the turn into Ferry Branch, and rowed straight for the sunken boats which blocked the channel to Baltimore harbor. Unfortunately for them, they were discovered by the men at Lazaretto and had to turn around and row back to the *Surprize.*

"The Bombardment of Fort McHenry", Alfred Jacob Miller   *Maryland Historical Society*

Unaware that he had lost half his flotilla, Napier led his remaining boats into Ferry Branch. Sticking close to the far shore he slipped safely by Fort McHenry. If he could ease past Fort Babcock too, he would be opposite Fort Covington, about where he should anchor.

But the plan was not to work. What was it that went wrong? Sailing Master John Webster, at Battery Babcock, later wrote, "Very soon after we would discern a small glimmering of light at different places. I was sure it must be the matches on board the enemy barges, . . . Some of the lights were above me next to Fort Covington." Reacting quickly, the batteries at Forts Babcock and Covington opened fire. It was returned by Napier. Then Fort McHenry itself joined in. So did the British ships from their positions well beyond the fort.

In the midst of the fiery fray, Napier began to worry. His orders had been to keep firing until he saw the army was "seriously engaged." But what now? It was after 3:00 A.M., and no hints of battle were coming from Hampstead Hill—no rumble of cannons, no flashes of powder, no shriek of rockets.

Something must have gone wrong there, too. Napier weighed the situation and came to the conclusion that to stay in Ferry Branch any longer could serve no conceivable purpose. He signaled his barges to turn around and begin the long row back.

But even the retreat was not to be without mishap. While attempting to slip

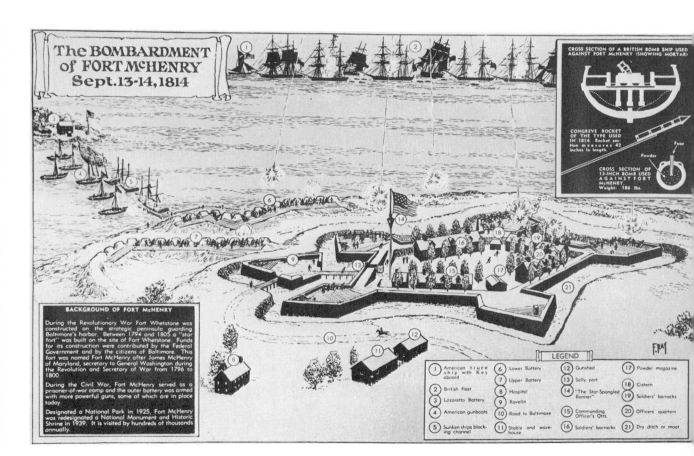

Bombardment of Fort McHenry

Frederic Ray

past Fort McHenry, one of Napier's men fired a signal rocket to let the fleet know they were returning. Naturally, it let the fort know, too, and Armistead's guns responded immediately with a torrent of balls and grapeshot.

Later, the British were to claim that only one life was lost and only one boat was "slightly struck" during Napier's foray. The Americans, however, found the remains of at least two boats and the bodies of three seamen.

By 4:00 A.M., Napier's boats were once again alongside the British ships and firing from the fort had come to an end. However, shots still came from the British vessels. Robert Barrett, a young English sailor, wrote later of the last hours of the battle: "The night was broken only by the firing of the bombs, as they continued with unremitting assiduity to hurl their destructive missiles on the foe."

While the English fleet was launching its attack upon Fort McHenry, Colonel Brooke and his troops remained bivouacked on the field of battle. On the morning of the 13th, they broke camp, formed for an attack, and made a feint to the north of the fortifications as though intending to turn the flank. There Brooke met a strong force under General Winder and was driven back. He next moved to within a mile of the fortifications and made a careful assessment of their strength in men and guns. Shortly thereafter, he decided that the American position could not be taken by storm.

Admiral Cochrane, of course, had arrived at the same decision concerning Fort McHenry on the morning of the 14th and had determined to suspend the attack of Baltimore altogether. Accordingly, a messenger was dispatched to Colonel Brooke advising him to move his troops back to the transports. No doubt Brooke followed the advice enthusiastically!

At 7:00 A.M., the *Surprize* signaled the bombarding squadron to return to North Point. By 8:00 the *Erebus* and the five bomb ships were under way, and at 9:00 the supporting frigates had begun to follow. Thus, Fort McHenry, by denying the British access to the North West Branch, had frustrated their strategy for the capture of Baltimore. The failure to take Baltimore greatly strengthened the position of the American peace negotiators at Ghent.

General Smith summarized the momentous events in only one sentence, part of a short letter he wrote to James Monroe, Acting Secretary of War, at 10:00 A.M. on the morning of the 14th, while he was still at his headquarters on Hampstead Hill.

"Sir," the letter began, "I have the honor of informing you that the enemy, after an unsuccessful attempt both by land and water, on this place, appears to be retiring."

Then, as though for good measure, he added a P.S. "The enemy's vessels in the Patapsco are all under way going down the river," he wrote. "I have good reason to believe that General Ross is mortally wounded."

Some time after the abortive invasion, Armistead estimated that the British had hurled between 1,500 and 1,800 shells at the fort; of those about 400 had landed within the defense works. Although two of the buildings were severely damaged and the others received slight injury, the casualty list was amazingly small. Of the 1,000 defenders, only four were killed and 24 injured. The appearance of the fort after the attack is briefly described in an entry of the Orderly Book of the Lebanon Blues, which mentions that:

> "The captain was at Fort McHenry and report it is all cut up round about it—he brought a piece of the bomb shell with him—he further says that there is some so large they weigh 200 lbs."

By a very curious coincidence, on September 13, 1814, the very day of the

Fort McHenry Rooster   *"Old Maryland"*

British attack, Colonel Jean Foncin wrote from Philadelphia to James McHenry in Baltimore. The purpose of his letter was to ask the former Secretary of War for a letter of recommendation, because "our French Government being returned to our old beloved sovereigns, and it is my duty to go back to my country." But, as something of an aside, he mentioned "the flattering rememberance of the satisfaction of the citizens of Baltimore, while I was building Fort McHenry." Then, in a postscript, he added:

> *"It is a painful idea to me, that the beautiful city of Baltimore be exposed to the disasters of War; but my mind will be a little solaced, if Fort McHenry does answer the purpose for which it was established, and affords me the satisfaction of having contributed to your defense."*

Soon after the battle, the heroes of the defense were honored throughout the city and presented with gifts for their bravery. Armistead was brevetted a Lieutenant Colonel on September 16, 1814.

One of the light-hearted incidents to arise from the otherwise grim bombardment did so in the form of a rooster. During the shelling, at a time when the fire was at its height, the bird jumped upon a parapet and crowed lustily. Its almost consciously defiant action helped to inspire the fort's defenders to renewed effort. Tradition has it that one soldier vowed he would treat the rooster to a pound cake if he lived to see Baltimore again. He did live, and he kept his word. The day after the bombardment, he sent into the city and procured the promised cake.

The legend goes on to relate that Colonel Armistead offered to purchase the rooster, but its owner would not part with it. Having been wounded by a bomb fragment, the rooster died a short time later. It was placed in a decorated wooden box and buried with full honors at Fort McHenry.

How was the bombardment seen from the city itself? There is much to be learned from the accounts of observers in the city. Annie Leakin Souissant, writing in *Old Baltimore,* relates that "One of the heroic women who stayed in the city when most of the other women and children had been removed wrote her personal recollections. The orders were, she said, that there was to be no light in town on any account, as lights would only serve to guide the fire of the enemy. The rain was falling heavily, and the darkness could almost be felt. Just before day dawned there was a scream of a shell from the fleet, and from that moment, 'it was like the very gate of Hell.'

"In the fort itself, a deadline had been drawn and orders given not to go beyond it, but one woman [who] had slipped in on some errand of supply in violation of these orders, was crossing the parade ground just as a shell hurtled in. It caught her and cut her in two."

Souissant continues, "James Ellicott, of Baltimore, described the events of September 14, in the following letter to his cousin in Batavia, New York, the morning after the bombardment:

'The bombardment of the fort was a scene interesting; terrible and grand. During the whole of last night we were able from the tops of the houses in town to trace every rocket and shell from the time it left the mortar until it struck or exploded in the air, but now my curiosity is perfectly satisfied with such scenes, and I have no wish that they should ever be resumed in this place for my amusement. It is supposed they threw 1,000 to 1,500 shells during the bombardment and with a precision utterly surprising.' "

In a report in *Niles Weekly Register,* the opinion was expressed that probably never before in any given time had so many rounds been fired in such close succession.

The successful defense of Baltimore was hailed with great delight throughout the country, and nervous Philadelphia and New York breathed more easily. To the British, the blow was humiliating, for expectations of success had been high throughout the realm. After the capture of Washington, that of Baltimore had seemed but holiday sport. In fact, the Governor General of Canada had been so sure of a victory by General Ross that, after the burning of Washington, he postponed proposed public rejoicings at Montreal until the "triumph" at Baltimore could be celebrated concurrently.

In England, no one had seemed to doubt that an army from Canada would meet Ross's troops on the Susquehanna or the Schuylkill River as conquerors of the country, and that Baltimore would be their base for future operations. "In the diplomatic circles it is rumored," said a London paper as early as June 17, "that our naval and military commanders on the American soil have no power to conclude any armistice or suspension of arms. They carry with them certain terms," the supercilious writer continued, "which will be offered to the American government at the point of a bayonet. There is reason to believe that America will be left in a much worse situation, as a naval and commercial power, than she was at the commencement of the war."

This program, so gratifying to British arrogance and British commerical greed, was not carried out. Instead of mourning as captives, Americans waxed jubilant as victors.

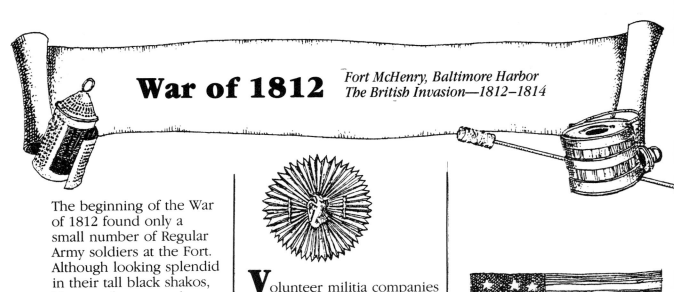

War of 1812

Fort McHenry, Baltimore Harbor
The British Invasion—1812–1814

The beginning of the War of 1812 found only a small number of Regular Army soldiers at the Fort. Although looking splendid in their tall black shakos, blue wool coats, and polished white belts, they were too few to defend the harbor.

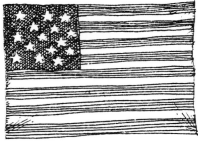

Volunteer militia companies arrived to assist the Army. Dressed in high fan shaped hats called Chapeau de Bras, and fancy wool coats of blue and red, they trained regularly to learn the hard work of soldiering.

Unemployed sailors were formed into companies of Sea Fencibles. Working beneath the Fort's huge 30 by 42 foot flag, they proved to be reliable gunners.

Large iron cannon were mounted on heavy wooden carriages. It was a dangerous task to ram the powder and iron ball down the barrel, take aim, and fire. The 1,000 men stationed at Fort McHenry were successful in driving off the British attack with these guns.

"THE STAR-SPANGLED BANNER" POEM AND FLAG

IF FORT MCHENRY has a place in American history because of the part it played in the defense of Baltimore and the nation during the War of 1812, it has a place in American hearts because of its role in the creation of our national anthem, "The Star-Spangled Banner."

The long series of events which eventually resulted in the writing of the famous poem began before the Battle of Baltimore—in August of 1814, when the British occupied Upper Marlboro shortly before the Battle of Bladensburg.

At Upper Marlboro, General Ross had set up temporary headquarters in the house of Dr. William Beanes, an elderly and respected physician. At that time, Beanes was required to render an oath of good behavior.

The British remained in Upper Marlboro only a short time. They returned, however, after the Battle of Bladensburg and the ensuing sack of Washington. When they did, they again inflicted themselves upon Dr. Beanes. Precisely what happened is not clear. Beanes family tradition has the doctor entertaining when the privacy of his home was shattered by the uninvited entrance of three rowdy British stragglers—stragglers who were summarily arrested and charged with disturbing the peace.

There are other accounts, though—and they are both British and American—which claim that Beanes headed a posse-like group which deliberately set out to find and capture British stragglers.

In any event, one of the three enemy soldiers who was in fact arrested at Upper Marlboro escaped, made his way back to his own troops, and reported the incident. The British naturally considered it a violation of the pledge of "good behavior" made to them by Dr. Beanes, and they arrested the physician forthwith. He was placed in the custody of an armed patrol, taken to the British base on the Patuxent, and turned over to Admiral Cochrane.

Word of Beanes' arrest spread quickly through the little town and efforts were begun to obtain his release. When they failed, Beanes' friends sought the assistance of one more influential than they: Francis Scott Key, an attorney who had been born on a landed estate in Western Maryland in 1779, had married into a prominant Eastern Shore family, and established a respectable practice of law in Georgetown, near Washington.

Key, also a friend of Dr. Beanes, accepted the plea of the doctor's neighbors. Yes, he would undertake to intercede in the old gentleman's behalf. Bearing official

Francis Scott Key—
Author of the Star-Spangled Banner
Maryland Historical Society

letters of introduction, he set off for Baltimore to join company with Colonel John Skinner, a federal agent whose job was arranging the transfer of prisoners.

On September 5, 1814, the two Americans sailed from Baltimore to rendezvous with the British fleet somewhere in the Cheaspeake Bay. The rendezvous occurred a little more quickly than Key and Skinner anticipated, for the fleet was on its way to Baltimore, bent on attack.

Historians Lessem and Mackenzie have described the meeting of Key, Skinner and Cochrane thusly:

> "Key and Skinner boarded the Tonnant, *flagship of the English fleet, where they were courteously received by Admiral Cochrane and General Ross and invited to dine in the admiral's cabin. After dinner was served, Key opened negotiations with the British for the release of Dr. Beanes. At first the English were adamant in their resolve to transport Beanes to Halifax where they intended to punish him for allegedly violating his oath of good behavior.*

> "During these early negotiations the Americans made little progress. Colonel Skinner, however, had carried with him a pouch of letters, written by British soldiers wounded at Bladensburg, extolling the excellent treatment they had received at the hands of the Americans. This information tended to mollify the stubborn attitude maintained by the British, and after a brief discussion Admiral Cochrane agreed to release Dr. Beanes.

> "However, Key and Skinner, who had become aware of the British plans for the attack on Baltimore, were informed that for security reasons they would not be allowed to return to Baltimore until the British objective had been attained. Since the H.M.S. Tonnant *was already overcrowded with British military personnel, the two Americans were transferred to the H.M.S. Surprize, a light frigate, where they remained until the fleet reached the mouth of the Patapsco."

The *Tonnant*, however, was a relatively large ship of 80 guns. It was of too deep a draft to negotiate the shallow waters of the upper Patapsco. Therefore, since Admiral Cochrane was determined to take personal charge of the attack on Fort McHenry, he was obliged to transfer his flag to the smaller *Surprize*. That, in turn, meant once again shifting Key and Skinner. This time their move was back to the American boat on which they had originally sailed from Baltimore. It was from that

Key sees "our flag is still there",
Percy Moran—Peale Museum

O say can you see, ~~through~~ by the dawn's early light,
What so proudly we hail'd at the twilight's last gleaming,
Whose broad stripes & bright stars through the perilous fight
O'er the ramparts we watch'd, were so gallantly streaming?
And the rocket's red glare, the bomb bursting in air,
Gave proof through the night that our flag was still there,
O say does that star spangled banner yet wave
O'er the land of the free & the home of the brave?

On the shore dimly seen through the mists of the deep,
Where the foe's haughty host in dread silence reposes,
What is that which the breeze, o'er the towering steep,
As it fitfully blows, half conceals, half discloses?
Now it catches the gleam of the morning's first beam,
In full glory reflected now shines in the stream,
'Tis the star-spangled banner — O long may it wave
O'er the land of the free & the home of the brave!

And where is that band who so vauntingly swore,
That the havoc of war & the battle's confusion
A home & a Country should leave us no more?
~~ ~~
Their blood has wash'd out their foul footstep's pollution.
No refuge could save the hireling & slave
From the terror of flight or the gloom of the grave,
And the star-spangled banner in triumph doth wave
O'er the land of the free & the home of the brave.

O thus be it ever when freemen shall stand
Between their lov'd home & the war's desolation!
Blest with vict'ry & peace may the heav'n rescued land
Praise the power that hath made & preserv'd us a nation!
Then conquer we must, when our cause it is just,
And this be our motto — "In God is our trust,"
And the star-spangled banner in triumph shall wave
O'er the land of the free & the home of the brave. —

vessel, at anchor somewhere downriver from the British fleet, that Key and his fellow Americans watched the bombardment of Fort McHenry.

At the end of the siege—after 25 hours of brutal pounding by bomb- and rocket-ships—Fort McHenry stood silent in the pre-dawn blackness. Key was breathless with anxiety. What had happened? What had been the outcome of the battle? As the first rays of dawn began to lighten the skies, as morning breezes began to clear the waters of mists and lingering rain clouds, Key once again directed his spyglass toward the fort in search of an answer. This time the answer was there—and what a glorious answer it was: the proud red, white, and blue of the Star-Spangled Banner, waving in triumphant victory high over its staunch star fort!

A combination of deep relief and patriotic fervor swept over Key. From his pocket he pulled an old letter. On its back he began to express his emotions in verse.

Many years later, in a speech delivered in his native Frederick County, he recalled his feelings at the time:

"I saw the flag of my country waving over a city—the strength and pride of my native State—a city devoted to plunder and desolution by its assailants. I witnessed the preparation for its assaults, and I saw the array of its enemies as they advanced to the attack. I heard the sound of battle; the noise of the conflict fell upon my listening ear, and told me that 'the brave and the free' had met the invaders.

"Through the clouds of the war the stars of that banner still shone in my view, and I saw the discomfited host of its assailants driven back in ignominy to their ships. Then, in that hour of deliverance and joyful triumph, my heart spoke; and 'Does not such a country and such defenders of their country deserve a song?' was its question. With it came an inspiration not to be resisted; and even though it had been a hanging matter to make a song, I must have written it. Let the praise, then, if any be due, be given, not to me, who only did what I could not help doing, not to the writer, but to the inspirers of the song."

On his return to Baltimore after the bombardment (with Skinner and Beanes, who had finally been released), Key sought the quiet of a room in the Indian Queen Hotel. There he revised and expanded his poem. The next morning, he showed it to Judge Joseph H. Nicholson, an in-law and friend. The judge was greatly impressed by the resounding lines of the poem and arranged to have it printed in handbill form by the *Baltimore American.* It was distributed to Baltimoreans on September 17, under the title "Defence of Fort McHenry." The introduction to the poem does not credit Key as its author, but refers to him as "a gentleman." (It was not until several weeks later that his name began appearing in connection with "The Defence of Fort McHenry.") On September 20, the poem was published in the *Baltimore Patriot.* Shortly thereafter, its title was changed to "The Star-Spangled Banner," by which it has been known ever since.

It is likely that Thomas Carr, a music publisher at 36 Baltimore Street, was the first to release the poem set to music. The tune with which it was paired was an old one, "To Anacreon in Heav'n."

Although many modern voices find the tune hard to carry because of its wide range, it does not seem to have presented any difficulties to folks of the 18th and early 19th centuries, to whom singing was a more commonplace pastime than it is today. The tune became so popular, in fact, that it was used with many different sets of words. In Ireland, it became a drinking song. In America a popular song, "Adams and Liberty," used the tune, and later, with a change of presidents, the tune became "Jefferson and Liberty." In all, it was adapted to more than 20 different songs. Brian

McGinty writes in *Early American Life*: " 'Anacreon' was an English song, but its geographic origins were never an important part of its appeal. It crossed the Atlantic to America some time in the 1780's and acquired a reputation of sorts even before it was made the subject of a host of popular parodies." The song was obviously familiar to Key—in 1805 he had composed such a parody himself, and it had, says McGinty, "included a line that strongly hinted at the immortal verse of 1814: 'By the light of the star-spangled flag of our nation.' "

Therefore, states McGinty, the words of "The Star-Spangled Banner" were "written for the music— . . . they were inspired, at least in part, by 'To Anacreon in Heav'n' itself." This piece of music had been written "about 1776 as the constitutional song of a gentlemen's club in London" which was called the Anacreontic Society. And, McGinty adds, "the words of 'Anacreon in Heav'n' were written by club president Ralph Tomlinson, a young solicitor of London, and set to music by the prominent composer, organist, and singer, John Stafford Smith."

As would be expected, "The Star-Spangled Banner" was an immediate "hit" in Baltimore and surrounding areas of Maryland. Its acceptance as the national anthem, however, was considerably slower. A milestone in that process occurred in 1889, when the song, already popular among the armed forces, was adopted by the Navy Department for playing at morning colors. In 1904, the Army instituted a similar procedure.

It took the First World War to give "The Star-Spangled Banner" such universal acceptance that a campaign could be mounted in Congress to make it the country's anthem. Still, official designation was not immediately forthcoming. A 1913 resolution was defeated; so was a 1918 bill which was introduced by Maryland Congressman J. Charles Linthicum.

Opposition to Linthicum's efforts (they were to last many years) came from many fronts: from the supporters of more "singable" songs such as *Yankee Doodle, Hail Columbia,* and *America the Beautiful;* from pacifists, who declared that "The Star-Spangled Banner" was too bellicose in spirit; and from temperance types who were simply aghast that an "Irish drinking song" might ever become the national anthem of *their* country.

But Congressman Linthicum persisted, introducing six more bills before Key's poem as set to Smith's music was finally, in 1931, declared to be the National Anthem of the United States of America.

To say something of the proponents of "The Star-Spangled Banner," they, too, were a mixed lot. In their forefront was Mrs. Reuben Ross Holloway, of Baltimore. She had been national president of the Daughters of 1812 from 1914 to 1920 and was a woman with some unshakable convictions. She opposed women's suffrage and jury duty for women on grounds that a woman's place was in the home!

That, however, did not prevent her from roaming the streets of Baltimore in her unusual hat (patterned after the shako worn by American soldiers in the War of 1812), making sure that flags were properly hung. Her respect for the prospective national anthem knew no bounds. She believed one should stand at attention when it was played, even if one heard it while taking a bath.

During the 1920s, the veterans of World War I began to build political power, and it was their support that turned the tide in Linthicum's favor.

At one point the Veterans of Foreign Wars delivered a petition in favor of "The Star-Spangled Banner" with 5,000,000 signatures. The bill was freed from committee and sent to the floor of the House. There the opposition caved in. No Congressman was then willing to go on record as opposing "The Star-Spangled Banner." In 1930 Linthicum's bill was passed unanimously. The next year the process was repeated in

DEFENCE OF FORT M'HENRY.

The annexed song was composed under the following circumstances—
A gentleman had left Baltimore, in a flag of truce for the purpose of getting released from the British fleet, a friend of his who had been captured
at Marlborough.—He went as far as the mouth of the Patuxent, and was
not permitted to return lest the intended attack on Baltimore should be
disclosed. · He was therefore brought up the Bay to the mouth of the Patapsco, where the flag vessel was kept under the guns of a frigate, and
he was compelled to witness the bombardment of Fort M'Henry, which
the Admiral had boasted that he would carry in a few hours, and
that the city must fall. He watched the flag at the Fort through the
whole day with an anxiety that can be better felt than described, until
the night prevented him from seeing it. In the night he watched the Bomb
Shells, and at early dawn his eye was again greeted by the proudly waving
flag of his country.

Tune—Anacreon in Heaven.

O! say can you see by the dawn's early light,
    What so proudly we hailed at the twilight's last gleaming,
Whose broad stripes and bright stars through the perilous fight,
    O'er the ramparts we watch'd, were so gallantly streaming?
And the rockets' red glare, the Bombs bursting in air,
Gave proof through the night that our Flag was still there;
      O! say does that star-spangled Banner yet wave,
      O'er the Land of the free, and the home of the brave?

On the shore dimly seen through the mists of the deep,
    Where the foe's haughty host in dread silence reposes,
What is that which the breeze, o'er the towering steep,
    As it fitfully blows, half conceals, half discloses?
Now it catches the gleam of the morning's first beam,
In full glory reflected new shines in the stream,
      'Tis the star spangled banner, O! long may it wave
      O'er the land of the free and the home of the brave.

And where is that band who so vauntingly swore
    That the havoc of war and the battle's confusion,
A home and a country, shall leave us no more?
    Their blood has washed out their foul footsteps pollution.
No refuge could save the hireling and slave,
From the terror of flight or the gloom of the grave,
      And the star-spangled banner in triumph doth wave,
      O'er the Land of the Free, and the Home of the Brave.

O! thus be it ever when freemen shall stand,
    Between their lov'd home, and the war's desolation,
Blest with vict'ry and peace, may the Heav'n rescued land,
    Praise the Power that hath made and preserv'd us a nation!
Then conquer we must, when our cause it is just,
And this be our motto—" In God is our Trust;"
      And the star-spangled Banner in triumph shall wave,
      O'er the Land of the Free, and the Home of the Brave.

Handbill distributed in Baltimore on September 17, 1814

National Park Service, Fort McHenry

Mrs. Reuben Ross Holloway,
Patriot and Advocate for
the Star-Spangled Banner

National Park Service,
Fort McHenry

the Senate.

But what of the *flag*—the Star-Spangled Banner itself?

Because of its deteriorated, shot-up condition, it has long been assumed that the Star-Spangled Banner now in the Smithsonian Institution is the same one which flew all night during the Fort McHenry bombardment.

Writes Lord, "But during that windy, rain-swept night, might Armistead have substituted his storm flag, then, in the early morning, again hoisted his big flag in triumph as the British retired?" Was it the storm-flag—and not its famous larger counterpart—that Francis Scott Key actually saw?

Lord quotes an account of the battle by a young British midshipman. Written by Robert J. Barrett, of the *Hebrus,* it appeared in the *United Service Journal* in April, 1841. Describing the squadron's withdrawal from Fort McHenry, Barrett recalled: "As the last vessel spread her canvas to the wind, the Americans hoisted a most superb and splendid ensign on their battery."

A June 7, 1981, Baltimore *Sun* article reports that Scott Sheads, Fort McHenry National Park ranger-historian, turned up a letter at the library of the University of Virginia about the bombardment.

"It was printed in the Yankee, *a Boston newspaper, which stated that it was written by one of the editors of the* Baltimore Patriot *to his friend in Boston, September 17, 1814 . . . Scott Sheads attributes it to Isaac Monroe, a Baltimore editor who lived at 62 North Liberty Street.*

"Monroe was a member of an elite volunteer military unit, the Baltimore Fencibles, an artillery outfit which had been mustered by Judge Joseph H. Nicholson.

"In his letter, Monroe related the roaring night behind the parapet of Fort McHenry when the enemy shelled the fort. 'Upward of 1,500 bombs fell in and about the Fort,' he wrote in a relatively detailed account of the evening's defense. The Fencibles helped to fight off a bomb ship that tried to enfilade the fort shortly after midnight but

was driven off when Nicholson's battery and others in the fort opened up with grape and canister shot . . . The bombardment was kept up with intensified fury, 'til dawn of day, when they appeared to be disposed to decline the unprofitable conflict.

" 'At this time our morning gun was fired, the flag hoisted, Yankee Doodle played, and we all appeared in full view of a formidable and mortified enemy, who calculated upon our surrender in 20 minutes after the commencement of the action.' "

Monroe's revelation gives a strong indication that the huge Star-Spangled Banner was actually not shown off until after the battle. Others have argued that on a rainy night a banner of such size would have soaked up water, weighed tons, and been utterly unable to fly and flourish. Smithsonian naval historian Harold Langley thinks a small storm flag flew through the night. "We know it rained," he says. "Any flag would have hung by the pole, waterlogged, and no one could have seen much of it. The flag that streamed out from the pole in the morning was dry. In size it was the equivalent of John Hancock's signature on the Declaration of Independence—run up as the garrison's nose-thumbing gesture."

The Flag displayed at the Charleston Navy Yard, Boston, Massachusetts on June 24, 1873
Burroughs Collection of the Bostonian Society, Old State House, Boston

"The story of the birth of our National Anthem has not been changed," Mr. Sheads went on to say in the *Sun* article; "only, perhaps, the clarity of factual events that were a part of the whole which inspired Francis Scott Key to write simply the words he felt in his heart."

History records what happened to the Star-Spangled Banner after the bombardment.

Lieutenant Colonel Armistead, who continued to command at Fort McHenry, was given the flag, or assumed possession of it. It was hoisted the day his daughter was born. Family lore has it that the flag was carried in Armistead's funeral procession in 1818, appeared at a reception at the fort for General Lafayette in 1824, and was sent—ironically—to England late in the Civil War for safekeeping.

Georgianna Armistead inherited the relic when her father died. Later, when she moved to New York with her husband, William Appleton, she took the flag along. After her death it went to her son Eben Appleton. He revered it, and brought it out of storage on the anniversaries of the bombardment. In 1876, he sent it to the Philadelphia Centennial Exhibition.

Then, in 1880, he brought it to Baltimore and, with a man named W. W. Carter, rode with it in a carriage in the city's sesquicentennial parade. An old letter tells that he was so moved with the response of the crowd to the flag that he cut three swatches from it and give them to Carter. Carter later presented those fragments to the Maryland Historical Society, which, in 1926, sent them to the Smithsonian Institution.

In 1907, Eben Appleton loaned the flag itself to the Smithsonian. Later, to the abiding sorrow of Baltimore's city fathers, he made the loan a gift. At that time, the flag's conservation was the charge of Theodore Belote, an assistant curator of history. Rita Adrosko, flaglady of the Smithsonian's textiles division, designed the conservation plan. Amelia Fowler and her assistants set to work at the Smithsonian to restore the flag. The women, sewing for six weeks, stitched it to a linen backing, their job being made exceedingly difficult because the original cloth had a tendency to fall to pieces. No attempt has ever been made to restore the fragments the historical society presented.

The project was begun in May, 1914, in the Chapel (now the Commons room) of the Smithsonian "Castle," and was completed as promised on June 30. The cost of the work was $1,243 ($500 to the needlewomen, $500 to Mrs. Fowler, and the rest for materials). Curator Belote said the flag "should now last for centuries and could be flown from any flagpole if necessary, without a particle of injury."

The curious red "V," stitched on as a patch to one of the banner's white stripes, was recently discovered to have a red "B" embroidered on it. It is a guess that the patch may cover Armistead's signature and a date which are said to have been put on the flag. We will never know, because the museum people would never countenance removing the patch for a look, any more than they would reweave the holes or bind up the tatters.

The flag was displayed in the Arts and Industries Building—except during World War II, when it was bundled into tarpaper for safekeeping in Luray Caverns—until the new building, The Museum of American History, was opened in 1965. For the new vertical installation, which finally got the banner into the field-left position specified by the Flag Code adopted in 1923, tapes were sewn onto the backing to equalize stress.

Other fragments, if they exist at all, must be scattered far and wide. Six pieces are on display in Mary Pickersgill's Flag House in Baltimore. They are the gift of Mr. and Mrs. A. D. Emmart. They were given to Mr. Emmart's father and uncle when

The Star-Spangled Banner today

they were children by Mary Bracken, an Irish maid in the family employ.

Family tradition holds that Mary had long before worked for Georgianna Armistead Appleton—and that Mrs. Appleton, dismayed by the shabby condition of the flag, had one day taken scissors and trimmed the edges. The scraps were given to Mary, along with a little lecture on their importance.

That these fragments are genuine there is little doubt because Mrs. Elizabeth M. Sewell, of the Flag House, took them to the Smithsonian—where, she says, they matched perfectly with the fading Stars and Stripes.

The Star-Spangled Banner which hangs in honored glory at the Smithsonian is one of America's most important historical relics. The setting dramatically displays the Star-Spangled Banner as what it indisputably is: a treasured symbol of Liberty, Freedom and Democracy.

The Flag House, home of Mary Pickersgill in 1813, now a National Historic Landmark.   *Flag House, Baltimore*

THE AFTERMATH:
HONOR AND PEACE

EVEN AS THE BRITISH ships sailed away, the Army began strengthening Fort McHenry. Brigadier General William Winder wrote on September 18, 1814, "There will be required to render the magazine here bomb-proof 192,000 bricks and 40 brick layers." The War Department notified General Smith the next day, "It will be proper that the Fort be made bomb-proof and that additional block houses be erected, it being understood that the requisite funds will be advanced to the Government by the City." Baltimore advanced the funds, and the new construction began to take shape. In May, 1815, Lieutenant Colonel Armistead wrote: "The work near Baltimore, Fort McHenry, is in a perfect state of repair as far as I can ascertain."

If anyone was in a position to assess the state of the fort, it was surely Colonel Armistead. He knew it so well that, even as the British fleet approached, it was he and he alone who realized that its magazine was not bomb-proof. It is a credit to his bravery that he neither revealed the fact to his men—doubtless fearing they would flee—nor decided to abandon the fort, an action which would have left the city without its chief bulwark of defense.

Even though Armistead survived the attack upon Fort McHenry, the stress wrought upon his nervous system by the bombardment and the burden of the secret he had borne eventually took their toll. He developed heart trouble, and, on April 25, 1818, he died. He was only 38 years old.

The following account of his funeral appeared in the *Baltimore Patriot* on April 27, 1818:

> "*Participation in the general grief; the Brigadier General Sterett ordered out the 3rd brigade to attend the funeral, which took place yesterday (Sunday) afternoon, with the honors of war—the procession of military and citizens was the most numerous ever witnessed in Baltimore—The Rev Clergy announced the mournful event to their respective congregations at the conclusion of the morning service. The churches were closed in the afternoon and a city's tears bore witness to the high estimation in which the deceased was held, as a man, a citizen and a soldier. A detachment of artillery was stationed on Federal Hill and fired two twenty-four pound cannon during the ceremonies. He is gathered to his father, and to the fathers of his country. He is promoted to higher honors than earth can bestow.*"

Colonel Armistead was buried in the St. Paul's graveyard, located at Redwood

Street near Fremont Avenue in Baltimore.

Fort McHenry surely deserved a happier day and it got one on October 7, 1824, when a gala reception was held there for General Marquis de Lafayette during his much heralded visit to Baltimore. The famed general arrived aboard the USS *United States,* which anchored just off the fort. The barge which carried him from the ship to the fort was handsomely cushioned and carpeted. At its bow was an eagle bearing in its beak this appropriate motto: "Welcome Lafayette to the land of the free and the home of the brave."

He was conducted from the barge to the reception tent by General Samuel Smith as the fort band played *Lafayette's March.* As he neared the tent, he was greeted by Governor Samuel Stevens, Jr., and Colonel John Eager Howard. After welcoming speeches by Governor Stevens and Colonel Howard, General Lafayette replied:

> *"The pleasure to recognize my beloved companions in arms; the sound of names whose memory is dear to me; this meeting under the consecrated tent where we so often have pressed around our paternal commander in chief; excite emotions which your sympathizing hearts will better feel than I can express. This Fort, also most nobly defended in the last war, while it brings the affecting recollection of a confidential friend in my military family, associates with the rememberance of the illustrious defense of another fort, in the Revolutionary War, by the friend now near me, General Sam Smith. It had been the lot of the Maryland Line to acquire glory, in instances of bad as well as good fortune, and to whom can I better speak of the glory of that line than in addressing Colonel Howard. My dear brother soldiers, my feelings are too strong for utterance. I thank you most affectionately."*

General Marquis de Lafayette   *Maryland Historical Society*

FORT M'HENRY, BALTIMORE, MARYLAND.

[For description, see page 397.]

Visitors to a Peaceful Fort McHenry in 1853

Maryland Historical Society

The American and Commercial Daily Advertiser of October 9, 1824, described the feeling of the assembly as General Lafayette spoke in the following manner: "When the voice of Lafayette was heard addressing his old and loved fellow-soldiers, the surcharged hearts of all present could no longer withstand the rush of the feelings which came over them. Tears flowed and sobs were heard in every direction and this was the language which interpreted the convulsive double grasp with which they welcomed him."

After the presentation and introductions were made, the general and his family were invited to the second tent, where an elegant meal in the French style was set out. The dinnerware used upon this occasion was a superb service which the city of Baltimore had presented to Colonel Armistead for his able defense of Fort McHenry during the bombardment. A gift was then presented to General Lafayette, which he received with great interest, and, one might suspect, with great reverence, for it was the camp chest of George Washington. It still contained the knives, plates, and other implements his dear friend had used.

As Lafayette left the fort, he noticed that on one side of the tent a French cannon had been mounted; on the other was an American cannon. Both had been used at the siege of Yorktown.

The next year, 1825, a German visitor, Karl Bernhard, the Duke of Saxe-Weimar Eisenach, described the fort in *Travels Through North American During the Years 1825 and 1826*. Undoubtedly influenced by the large fortresses of Europe, he found Fort McHenry unimpressive. Yet he was an accurate observer:

"The fort itself is very small, and ill-shaped; a pentagon with five little bastions, where at most but three large guns can be mounted; in front of the entrance is a little ravelin which defends nothing. There is no counterscarp; the ramparts are sodded. The fort is separated from the land by a wall, which might rather prove injurious than advantageous. Near the water's edge there is a battery which can contain more than fifty guns for firing over the beach. There are also some furnaces for heating cannon balls. It was this battery which offered the greatest resistance to the British. Since that time, the engineers have erected bomb-proofs on each side of the gate, as well as a bomb-proof powder magazine. . ."

For the next nine years there was very little money appropriated for maintenance, and the buildings in the fort began to deteriorate. Lieutenant Henry Thompson, Corps of Artillery, arrived at Fort McHenry in the fall of 1833. Besides being the nephew of General Gratiot, Chief of Engineers in Washington, he was an accomplished artist and a competent supervisor of construction.

During the next six years, Thompson supervised considerable improvements, repairs and new fortification construction, first as an army officer, then, after his resignation in 1836, as a civil superintendent. On occasion he prepared excellent drawings of the fort for the benefit of his uncle in Washington.

In 1839, Baltimore lost another of its gallant 1814 defenders: Sam Smith.

"Another patriot gone!" April 27th's *Niles' National Register* lamented. The journal went on to report:

"General Samuel Smith, of Baltimore . . . died in that city on Monday afternoon last, in the 87th year of his age. He had been riding in his carriage, and on his return to his dwelling, laid upon the sofa with the view of resting himself, and when the servant who had been attending him entered the apartment a short time afterwards, he was found dead. His career was glorious and useful, and he has died full of years and honor . . . When Baltimore was threatened with foreign invasion, he accepted the command of the defending army, and pledged his own private fortune . . . During the whole term of his command here, neither he nor his staff received any pay. . ."

As fate would have it, Fort McHenry "died" shortly after General Smith did. Great changes in warfare and weaponry—more powerful cannons, propellents and projectiles—had rendered it obsolete. In addition, the rapid postwar expansion of Baltimore's harbor below the fort minimized the strategic importance of Whetstone Point. Thus, it was not surprising that, in the mid-1840s, the War Department decided to build a new fort four and a half miles below Fort McHenry.

In 1847, Sollers Flats, an island of four acres lying between Sparrows and Hawkins Points, was transferred to the federal government for the purpose of erecting the new fort. Work commenced on March 1, 1848, under the command of Major Cornelius A. Ogden. On November 15, he was relieved by a brevet colonel of engineers. The relieving officer was none other than Robert E. Lee, who, in 1848, was a graduate of West Point and a veteran of the war with Mexico.

The original specifications called for a six-sided structure with walls eight to ten feet thick, capable of withstanding shell fire for a protracted period. It was also to contain gun emplacements for 350 pieces of ordnance and have sufficient ranging stations and watch towers. Within were to be ammunition arsenals, quarters for men and officers, and adequate water supplies.

Fort Carroll

A. Aubrey Bodine

For the next three years, Colonel Lee lived with his family at 908 Madison Avenue, a three-story brick row house across the street from Mt. Calvary Church, near Hamilton Terrace. It was a happy period for him; he had relatives in Baltimore and enjoyed a pleasant social life.

In 1850, the new fort was named Fort Carroll, in honor of Charles Carroll of Carrollton, the Marylander who, before his death in 1832, had been the last surviving signer of the Declaration of Independence.

By the end of four years, however, the War Department had begun to lose interest in the Baltimore project. Appropriations were made more and more slowly. On May 27, 1852, Colonel Lee was ordered to West Point to become the Military Academy's ninth superintendent. Later that same year, Congress failed to appropriate new funds for the fort, and, under Lee's successors, work lagged. A ring of gun embrasures was completed, with brick magazines, storerooms, and troop quarters, but the entire structure was found to be settling, and work stopped.

Although Fort McHenry's strategic role was declining, its regular garrison remained. In addition, the fort became a recruit depot in late 1846. During the Mexican War (1846–1848), Maryland troops were trained there before being sent to the Southwest. It was not until the tragedy of the Civil War that Fort McHenry was called upon to play another role of real significance in the life of its city and nation.

Colonel Robert E. Lee.

CIVIL WAR YEARS

"The *land of the free . . ."*

Those words from our nation's anthem come to the mind of every visitor to Fort McHenry.

Few visitors realize, however, that during the Civil War Fort McHenry was a place where the treasured concept of political freedom was mocked. It was, as many observers have pointed out, an "American Bastille."

In 1860, the year immediately preceding the war, events occurred at a furious pace. The secession of the Southern States continued as flames of emotion rose on both sides and efforts to bring about a peaceful reconcilliation became more and more ineffectual. In Baltimore, the occurrences were watched with intense interest. The majority of Baltimoreans sympathized with the South, but scarcely more than a handful advocated the secession of Maryland. Devotion to the Union under the Constitution was the dominant sentiment. As events hurried on, however, the division of sympathies became more and more pronounced, and the citizenry began to side with North or South.

At a late hour on Friday, April 12, 1861, a dispatch was received from Charleston, South Carolina, announcing that an attack on Fort Sumter had begun. This news was received in Baltimore with excitement which waxed even more intense when it was learned that neighboring Virginia had joined the secessionists on April 17.

At noon on April 18, a mob of Southern supporters tramped up Federal Hill with a flagpole, a Confederate flag, and a cannon. They hoisted the flag and began firing a salute of 100 guns, but a band of Union supporters stormed the hill and drove the rebel sympathizers off. In short order the rebel flag was burned, and the cannon was cast into the Basin.

The next day—one of the darkest days in the history of Baltimore—a mob attacked the soldiers of the 6th Massachusetts Regiment as they marched from the President Street railroad station along Pratt Street to the Camden station. Four of the Massachusetts regiment were killed, and 36 were wounded. Twelve citizens were killed; the number of wounded has never been ascertained. As the fighting was at close quarters, the small number of casualties shows that it was not so severe as has generally been supposed. Nonetheless, the North's reaction to the "Baltimore Massacre" was vituperative. Newspapers there called for blood—Baltimore's.

An editorial in the New York *Tribune* read in part:

The Fort, 1861, from Lazaretto Lighthouse

"One section of the country is only semi-civilized. In a society so constituted it is not strange that there should be found many persons who could conceive and execute some diabolical plot of slaughter."

The Boston *Courier* called upon the men of Massachusetts to "organize and push on to Baltimore to lay it in ashes." Bostonians, incensed by the attack on the 6th Massachusetts Regiment, began to sing:

"There's swelling cry for vengeance on the counterfeits of men who haunt that hold of pirates—that foul assassin's den!"

Meanwhile, in Baltimore itself, excitement and alarm were spreading. The following item, taken from the *American* of April 22, describes the grave situation in the city at that time.

"War Spirit on Saturday"

"The war spirit raged throughout the city and among all classes during Saturday with an ardor which seemed to gather fresh force each hour . . . All were united in a determination to resist at every hazard the passage of troops through Baltimore . . . Armed men were marching through the streets, and the military were moving about in every direction, and it is evident that Baltimore is to be the battlefield of the Southern revolution."

That very morning Captain John C. Robinson, commander at Fort McHenry, wrote to Colonel L. Thomas, Adjutant-General of the United States Army, that, because of the hostile mood of many Baltimoreans, he was sure he would be attacked that night. He was equally sure, he added, that he could hold the fort for the Union.

Robinson's confidence was verified by the following report which appeared in *Baltimore American and Commerical Advertizer:*

> *"Since the commencement of actual hostilities between the North and the South, Fort McHenry has become an object of special attraction on the part of the citizens of Baltimore. The post is under the command of Captain Robinson, of the Fifth Infantry, who is universally esteemed as an accomplished and experienced officer. The fort has not been reinforced, the rumors to the contrary notwithstanding, the number of effective men is about two hundred, who are kept in a high state of military discipline. The strictest military regulations are necessarily enforced, and citizens are not admitted within the works."*

On the morning of the 21st, Captain Robinson gave the following report of the apprehended attack on the fort, and the conduct of the Baltimore authorities:

> *"About nine o'clock on the evening of the 20th, Police Commissioner Davis called at the fort, bringing a letter, dated eight o'clock p.m. of the same evening, from Charles Howard, the president of the board, which he quotes at length, and which*

5th Massachusetts Regiment faces hostile reception on Pratt Street, April 19, 1861   *Maryland Historical Society*

states that, from rumors that had reached the board, they were apprehensive that the commander of the fort might be annoyed by lawless and disorderly characters approaching the walls of the fort, and they proposed to send a guard of perhaps two hundred men to station themselves on Whetstone Point, of course beyond the outer limits of the fort, with orders to arrest and hand over to the civil authorities any evil-disposed and disorderly persons who might approach the fort. The letter further stated that this duty would be confided to the police force, but their services were so imperatively required elsewhere that it would be impossible to detail a sufficient number, and this duty had therefore been entrusted to a detachment of the regular organized militia of the State, then called out pursuant to law, and actually in the service of the State. It was added that the commanding officer of the detachment would be ordered to communicate with Captain Robinson. A postscript stated that there might perhaps be a troop of volunteer cavalry with the detachment.

"I did not question the good faith of Mr. Howard, but Commissioner Davis verbally stated that they proposed to send the Maryland Guards to help protect the fort. Having made the acquaintance of some of the officers of that organization, and heard them freely express their opinions, I declined the offered support, and then the following conversation occurred:

"Commandant: I am aware, sir, that we are to be attacked tonight. I received notice of it before sundown. If you will go outside with me you will see we are prepared for it. You will find the guns loaded, and men standing by them. As for the Maryland Guards, they cannot come here. I am acquainted with some of those

gentlemen, and know what their sentiments are.

"Commissioner Davis: *Why, Captain, we are anxious to avoid a collision.*

"Commandant: *So am I, sir. If you wish to avoid a collision, place your city military anywhere between the city and that chapel on the road, but if they come this side of it, I shall fire on them.*

"Commissioner Davis: *Would you fire into the city of Baltimore?*

"Commandant: *I should be sorry to do it, sir, but if it becomes necessary in order to hold this fort, I shall not hestiate for one moment.*

"Commissioner Davis (*excitedly*): *I assure you, Captain Robinson, if there is a woman or child killed in that city, there will not be one of you left alive here, sir.*

"Commandant: *Very well, sir, I will take the chances. Now I assure you, Mr. Davis, if your Baltimore mob comes down here tonight you will not have another mob in Baltimore for ten years to come, sir.*"

The Secretary of War must have shared Captain Robinson's fears, for he sent three regiments of Philadelphia troops, under the command of General George Cadwallader. As soon as General Cadwallader relieved General Benjamin Butler as commander of the Maryland district, he divided his troops between Federal Hill and Fort McHenry. He and his staff made their headquarters at Fort McHenry. Captain Robinson was given a command in the field, and Major W. W. Morris was named commandant of Fort McHenry.

1814 Battle Monument is scene of arrival of Cook's Boston Light Infantry, July 1861   *Maryland Historical Society*

But an attack never came, either from "the hold of pirates" or from Confederate forces. No, during the Civil War, Fort McHenry was indeed to become America's Bastille.

As early as June, 1861, the head of the Baltimore police force, Marshall George Kane, was arrested and confined at the fort simply because the Union forces could not tolerate the direction of such a large number of armed men being in the hands of a person whose loyalty they suspected. When the Board of Police Commissioners met to consider the arrest of Kane, they refused to approve. For their lack of compliance, they, too, were arrested and sent to the fort.

During the summer of 1861, Maryland's Governor, Thomas Holliday Hicks, himself opposed to secession, had ordered the General Assembly to meet in Frederick because Annapolis, the state capital, was occupied by Federal troops. The governor's decision may also have been influenced by the knowledge that public opinion was more pro-Union in the Frederick area than it was in Eastern and Southern Maryland. Be that as it may, the legislators never had the opportunity to vote a clear "yes" or "no" on secession because the anti-secession minority, by cleverly absenting themselves during quorum counts, managed to postpone a vote until the question was moot.

Still, it was quite clear that some members of the General Assembly would be satisfied only when Maryland withdrew from the Union; it was decided that those gentlemen must be arrested. Allen Pinkerton, the head of the Union spy network, was summoned to Baltimore to perform this task. Fort McHenry became his headquarters and from there he made his raids into Baltimore City. By an unhappy coincidence, Pinkerton and his men went into Baltimore on September 13—the 47th anniversary of the bombardment of the fort—to arrest the members of the General Assembly. Pinkerton's group were successful, and when they returned to the fort they also had Mayor George Brown in custody. He, too, had been arrested for his secessionist leanings.

Ironically, also arrested on that day were George Armistead Appleton, grandson of Lieutenant Colonel George Armistead, the hero of the bombardment at the fort (for carrying a Confederate flag in his possession), and Francis Key Howard, grandson of the lawyer-poet who just 47 years earlier had penned "The Star-Spangled Banner." Howard was arrested for being one of the editors of the *Baltimore Exchange*, a newspaper with leanings sympathetic to the South.

Howard's first night at Fort McHenry was described in John A. Marshall's *American Bastille:*

"I reached Fort McHenry about two o'clock in the morning. There I found several of my friends and others were brought in a few minutes later. Among them were most of the members of the Legislature from Baltimore, Mr. Brown, the Mayor of the city, and one of our representatives in Congress, Mr. May. They were all gentlemen of high social position and of unimpeachable character. Each of them had been arrested, as has been said, solely on account of his political opinions, no definite charge having been then or afterward preferred against them. Two small rooms were assigned us during our stay. In the smaller one of these I was placed, with three companions. The furniture consisted of three or four chairs and an old rickety bedstead, upon which was the filthiest apology for a bed I ever saw. There was also a tolerably clean-looking mattress lying in one corner. Upon this mattress and upon the chairs and bedstead, we vainly tried to get a few hours sleep. The rooms were in the second story of the building, and opened upon a narrow balcony, which we were allowed to use, sentinels, however, being stationed on it. When I looked out in the morning, I could

Mayor George Brown   *Eric Davis*

Frank Key Howard   *Eric Davis*

Severn Teackle Wallis   *Eric Davis*

Marshall George P. Kane
        Dan Toomey

General John Adams Dix,
Commander of Union Forces
in Maryland   *Dan Toomey*

General William Morris,
Commander of Fort McHenry
        Eric Davis

not help being struck by an odd and not pleasant coincidence. On that day, forty-seven years before, my grandfather, Mr. Francis Scott Key, then a prisoner on a British ship, had witnessed the bombardment of Fort McHenry. When, on the following morning, the hostile fleet drew off, defeated, he wrote the song so long popular throughout the country, the Star-Spangled Banner. As I stood upon the very scene of that conflict, I could not but contrast my position with his, forty-seven years before. The flag which he had then so proudly hailed, I saw waving, at the same place, over the victims of as vulgar and brutal a despotism as modern times have witnessed."

A few days later, Francis Key Howard, George Armistead Appleton, and a number of other political prisoners were transferred to Fortress Monroe, Virginia. Many of these gentlemen would not be released and returned to their homes in Baltimore until November of 1862. (Although there were some exceptions, most of Fort McHenry's political prisoners were quickly transferred to other Federal prisons.)

Baltimoreans watched these proceedings with feelings of helplessness engendered by the federal military presence throughout their city—not only at Fort McHenry, but

July 13, 1861, Columbiads at Fort McHenry, pointing to Washington Monument and to the City of Baltimore
Maryland Historical Society

also atop Federal Hill, and on the grounds of Mount Clare, Patterson Park and elsewhere. It was a presence which could not be ignored, as a delegation of ladies discovered when they visited the fort to lodge a protest with General John Adams Dix, Commander of the Department of Maryland who had relieved General Cadwallader. This confrontation is recorded in *Memoirs of John Adams Dix:*

"The Baltimore women were received with the courtesy which the General usually displayed in his dealings with the fair sex. After some conversation, however, he invited them to walk around the walls. At a certain point they came upon an immense columbaid, the largest in the fort. Here the General stopped and said: 'Ladies, there will be no trouble in the city unless it is created by persons of your own social position;

the common people will not rise until they see the aristocracy of Baltimore moving. The safety of the town and the lives of its citizens are, therefore, substantially in your hands. Will you oblige me by mounting these steps, looking over the top of that gun, and noting the place which it points.' The ladies complied, and one exclaimed, 'It points to Monument Square.' 'Yes,' replied the General, 'and I now tell you that, if there should be an uprising in Baltimore, I shall be compelled to try to put it down; and that gun is the first that I shall fire.' "

Needless to say, there was no uprising in Baltimore, and Fort McHenry continued—unstormed, as it were—in its role of Bastille.

As surprising as it may seem in light of the terrible stories that have come from Andersonville and other Civil War prisons, some of Fort McHenry's political prisoners fared very well, especially when their treatment is compared to that recieved by the Federal and Confederate soldiers who were confined there. Consider, for example, the experience of Benjamin T. Gunter, a lawyer from Accomack County, Virginia, who was arrested on December 8, 1861, for visiting Richmond. As he recorded in his diary:

"December 12, 1861—At 10 o'clock the steamer reached Fort McHenry and I was handed over to Captain J. E. Mulford who took me to the room where I was to be confined. The prison is a room about 24 feet long by 15 feet wide, the back part of the room is elevated about 10 inches higher than the front. In the center of the room is an old fashioned tin plate wood stove which makes the room very comfortable, on the left as you enter is a small shelf for the water pitcher and in the right corner is a large tub. The room has two small windows on the left and right as you enter and these windows are guarded by iron bars. In the back of the room is an open window about 8 inches by 30 inches and this has four upright rods of iron. The furniture of the room consists of one small writing table, one chair, one Camp Set, two pitchers, one wash bowl and a bucket for the dirty water. Each prisoner is furnished with one army blanket and some got two. I am one of the fortunate ones. In front of this room is a pavement about 23 feet long and 9 feet wide upon which the prisoners are allowed to walk during the day. At sunset the door of this prison is locked after calling the roll of prisoners, and sunrise the door is again opened. I was then introduced to my four cellmates; H. W. Habersham, Annapolis, Md., B. Gibson, Talbot County, Md., John Davis, Annapolis, Md., and Richard T. Hardesty, Davidsonville, Md. It is a privilege allowed the prisoners to subscribe to any papers they see proper and Habersham being a subscriber to the Maryland News sheet so we will have the opportunity of reading this newspaper every morning.

"December 25, 1861—Soon after breakfast in walks Billy Neak whose residence is No. 40 Church Street—Federal Hill. Billy brings along with him a basket containing spoons, tumblers, eggs, sugar and a bottle together with a lot of stationery and a chair. Now for a merry Christmas, Habersham, we will have egg nog. Soon after I see a gentleman enter basket in hand: Who is that? O! it is our old friend W. W. Glenn; he never forgets us. Mr. Glenn came about 10 o'clock, bringing along with him a basket full of nice things—Turkey, Jelly, etc. etc. Who can those ladies be? said I to myself as I saw the ladies enter the fort, followed by two soldiers with baskets, and escorted, they cannot be some ministering angels. It is indeed true thought I to myself as I walked over to my room, and found them sitting around our cheerful fire, with those baskets sitting upon our table. I met Habersham at the door, and by him was introduced to these ladies—first Mrs. Charles Howard, Mrs. Murdock and Mrs. John Wight. The baskets brought were loaded down with the nicest delicacies of the season.

Among these things were a fire baked turkey, boiled ham, fruit cake, sponge cake, sugar cake, beef tongue, raisin pudding, canvasback duck, canned tomatoes, apples, pickles etc. etc. After my return from church I found Habersham busy making a bowl of eggnog so I rolled up my sleeves and went at it and soon we had a bowl of nice eggnog and now for Christmas. We invited a number of our friends to partake with us and we emptied the bowl in short order. After dinner we were sitting in our room having a smoke when we heard a rap on the door. As I opened the door I spied a large finely dressed, genteel looking Mulatto, Edward Sythe. When he came in he inquired for Habersham and said that for Mrs. Warfield and others, he had brought Habersham and others, whom she did not know, some things for Christmas. He apologized for their being cold and said he had hoped and expected to get them here warm. Among the delicacies were nice fried oysters, baked turkey, beef steak, bread, cake, celery, potatoes, two bottles of eggnog and a bottle of good whiskey. These we divided with our old friends in the other quarters.

"January 1, 1862—About 12 o'clock today I saw two gentlemen come walking in the fort, one with a little basket with something covered by a clean nice white towel. He came by our door and one of the gentlemen inquired for Mr. Gunter, when I informed him that I was the gentleman, and invited them to walk in, When they

Fort McHenry 1861

entered one of the gentlemen introduced himself to us as Mr. Lloyd W. Williams and also introduced the other gentleman as Colonel M. I. Cohen. I then introduced them to Lieutenant Habersham. They informed me that hearing that I was here they had come to pay me a visit and see if there was anything they could do for me or the other prisoners—or if there was anything we needed, and Colonel Cohen took out two bottles of very old whiskey, and two bottles of wine—one imported in 1829 the other in 1830, and presented them to me. Colonel Cohen is a tall fine looking old gentleman of 66 or 65 years of age and was in this fort in charge of a battery at the storming by the British in the war of 1812.

"As we were going out with these gentlemen, we saw three ladies coming in with a servant and two baskets. Who on earth can these be said I to myself? Soon I discovered it was our lady friends, Mrs. Howard, Mrs. Murdock and Mrs. Wight who paid us a visit on Christmas day and who had again come to pay us a New Year's visit. These ladies brought with them everything they could imagine we desired."

Mr. Gunter went on to record that the ladies, with the help of their servant, prepared and served an unforgettable New Year's day dinner which featured all the delicacies of the season. The feast started with a number of champagne toasts and ended when the ladies served each man a glass of brandy and his choice of a cigar or

Maryland Historical Society

pipe of tobacco.

But to return to Mr. Gunter's diary:

"Monday, January 6, 1862—At 10 o'clock Lieutenant Habersham and I, carpet bag in hand, started for the city to spend our 24-hour pass. We walked to Locust Point, then took the ferry across the river, and then by the cars we went to Barnum's City Hotel. While in town we called upon those of our friends who had visited us at the fort and during the day I stopped at Lanscheimers & Company to have clothes made and attended to other matters of business. At night by invitation we took tea at Mrs. Glenn's. After tea we went to the Front Street Theatre to see the celebrated ballet dancer, Cubas, and were disappointed in her performance—instead of being the beautiful Cubas as she is styled, she has no pretentions to beauty. On returning to Barnum's at 11 PM from the theatre we took a warm bath and went to bed. It was altogether a very agreeable day we had enjoyed, after being locked up for four weeks."

But not all of Fort McHenry's political prisoners were as lucky as the be-gifted Mr. Gunter. *American Bastille,* for instance, records the case of The Reverend Robert Douglas, an elderly minister whose Washington County farm, Ferry Hill Place, lay along the Confederate line of retreat after the Battle of Sharpsburg.

Known to be a man with Southern sympathies and the father of a member of General "Stonewall" Jackson's personal staff, the "Old Rebel Preacher," as he was derisively called, received no mercy from the Federal troops who had encamped on Ferry Hill Place.

All the crops of the season were taken without compensation, without even the pretense of military seizure. Tents were pitched in the yard, cannons planted about the house, and the inmates reduced to a state of siege. The battle having increased the animosity among citizens of opposite sympathies, frequent reports were made to headquarters about the rank disloyalty of the "Old Rebel Preacher"—specifically that he was in underground and treasonable communication with the Confederate general.

When, during a stormy night, a gust of wind blew open a bedroom shutter, allowing a beam of lamplight to flash out toward the Confederates, the spurious suspicions were confirmed. A watchful sentinal spotted the flash, and hastened to report that a signal light had been given from the house of the "Old Rebel." In the words of Mr. Marshall, it was "a grievous charge," and more grievously did the Reverend Mr. Douglas answer for it.

As Mr. Marshall wrote: "The next evening, without warning or reason, Reverend Douglas was taken from his home and family and marched to the quarters of General Fitz-John Porter. He requested an interview with the General, but was refused and sent immediately to Berlin, below Harper's Ferry. Here, in the open air, without shelter or any covering but the cloak he wore, and forbidden the use of fire, the old prisoner passed that cold and dreary night upon the frozen ground . . . And when, after the long night, the light of day appeared again, it witnessed the sad spectacle of the white hair of the old preacher mingling with the snow that lay all about him. A second and third night was spent in the same manner, except that a subordinate officer, whose heart was not steeled against compassion, declared that his treatment was a disgrace and gave him one of his own blankets to lie upon.

"After a few days," continues Marshall, "he was taken before General Burnside, where the oath of allegiance was offered him as the price of his release. This he declined . . . [instead he] demanded an investigation of the charges against him. His request was in turn disregarded, and he was hurried away to Fort McHenry."

On arrival at the Fort, Marshall writes, "He was shut up in what had been a horsestable, with deserters, criminals in ball-and-chain, and prisoners of the lowest grade . . . And yet—his age, appearance, and character had their effect even upon the wretches who surrounded him. They soon began to regard him with kindness and consideration. A fellow-prisoner thus describes Reverend Douglas's situation at that time and in that place:

> " 'A large number of prisoners, perhaps four hundred, occupied the hay-loft, and a larger number the stables below. After having seen Captain Barlow in regard to my quarters, and securing certain privileges for myself, he remarked to me that they were having a lively time in the front stable. An old grey-haired man [was] in there preaching to the soldiers, and he seemed to understand his business. He added that it was a bitter shame to have that old Christian gentlemen in there, but that he could not help it. He was charged with giving signal-lights to the rebels; he (Captain Barlow) did not believe it, but General Morris did, and there was no use in trying to get him out. He asked me to look through the bars and see if I knew the prisoner. He was holding service. At its conclusion, I looked in and saw him seated upon a board, and when he arose and approached, I at once recognized him, and we shook hands. We had some conversation, and as we parted he said in a full, earnest voice: "They may put me in prison; they may confine my body; but they cannot imprison my spirit and my soul. I have plenty of work in here for my Master, and, by his grace, I intend to do." He constantly held prayer in that stable, and his fellow-prisoners, as far as I could ascertain, exercised toward him the greatest affection and reverence.' "

Soon after, according to Mr. Marshall, by the order of the Provost Marshall, The Reverend Mr. Douglas was taken from the horsestable and placed in somewhat more comfortable quarters, with other state prisoners. While he remained with those kind gentlemen, they resolved that he should be as their guest, and should perform none of the duties of their prison life. His health, however, rapidly declined.

After he had been in confinement about six weeks, he was taken before the Provost Marshal, who treated him with much courtesy and ascertained, after an examination, that there was no evidence against him, and that no written charges had ever been preferred. He had been arrested and imprisoned on suspicion, prejudice, and the vaguest rumors. Feeble and sick, but a shadow of his former self, the "Old Rebel" was released and permitted to return to his home, where, after a few more years of preaching, he died on August 20, 1867.

The case of another man—a *real* spy, this one—reveals yet another manner in which prisoners were treated at Fort McHenry. His name was Henry Hall Brogden, and he was a Confederate captain who had been captured May 3, 1863, while crossing the Patuxent River. His account of his stay at Fort McHenry was recorded in his diary:

> "The cell in which I was confined was three feet wide by six feet long, but was ten or twelve feet high. It was under the parapet, in the casemate, and consequently underground. There was no window and no means of ventilation. It lay at the upper end of a narrow passage-way on which two other cells opened. The passage was entered through a small door at the lower end and from the guard room, so it can easily be seen that there was no light at the upper end of the passage where my cell was.
> "There was a grated iron door, which was closed all day, and there was a solid wooden door which was closed when the flag fell in the evening, and opened at guard mount in the morning. There was no bedstead or chair, there being no room for such luxuries. I was allowed a mattress, which I placed on the damp floor at

night, and stood up on end against the wall in the day. I was not allowed bed linen. At no time were the walls of my cell dry, the rear wall particularly. Moisture trickled down it the whole time, and I could fill my hand with a green slime, simply by passing it up the face of the wall.

"I was not allowed knife and fork, my food being cut up by the sentry outside and pushed through the grated door while I held a tin plate to catch it. I do not remember that the plate was washed during the entire time of my imprisonment in the cell. A tin basin, filled with water, was brought into the cell when the cleaning (so called) was done each morning, about eight o'clock, but there was no towel.

"There was no convenience for bathing, nor did I take a bath during the entire time of my confinement at the Fort. The sanitary arrangements consisted of a half-barrel, which was emptied in the morning, when the cell was cleaned. I was not allowed to leave my cell for any purpose except to confer with my lawyer or to see members of my family, and this I could only do in the presence of an officer, usually General Morris himself. As these visits did not occur often, a week or ten days would frequently elapse without my seeing the light of day.

"I was brought to trial in October, on the charge of being a spy. From the opening of the trial I was hopeless. It was a foregone conclusion, notwithstanding the brave manly fight made by Mr. Andrew Sterritt Ridgely, in my defense. The decision was 'guilty'.

"I was returned to the cell to await the carrying out of the sentence. I was too young to die—and such a death. I can convey no idea of what my feelings were at this time, nor is it pleasant to dwell on them now, except that it gives me pleasure to recall the fact that at no time did I break down.

"Time went on, and finally I was notified that the President had not approved the findings of the Commission, and that I was to be tried on another charge, that of having violated the 100th article of war, which prohibited coming within the Union lines without permission, and notwithstanding the fact that I was captured three days prior to the publication of the article referred to, I was convicted and sentenced to Sing Sing, or such military prison as the Secretary of War might select, for fifteen years.

"In December an order came from Washington to send me to Fort Delaware, and a few days after I bade farewell to my cell and have never seen it since. It will thus be seen that I was confined in the cell from the middle of May until the end of December.

"I went into the cell as a boy; I came out a gray-haired man with life-long experience."

On June 4, 1864, Captain Henry Hall Brogden was sent to Fortress Monroe and exchanged for a Captain Scott, a Union soldier who had been held as hostage for him.

Early in 1863, the war's middle years, Fort McHenry's prisoner population stood at some 800. These included 400 federal soldiers guilty of misconduct, 250 captured Confederate troops, and 30 civilians accused of such activities as privateering, recruiting for the Confederacy, or smuggling recruits across the Potomac River. But that was before Gettysburg.

After that bloody battle, fought in July of 1863, the number of prisoners soared to 6,957. The sick and wounded so strained the fort's hospital that some were cared for in tents adjacent to the Army general hospital which had been set up at Union dock in Baltimore. Within the fort, every building was jammed, all available extra tents were erected, and still hundreds of prisoners were without shelter. But, as Fort McHenry was primarily a transfer facility, the prisoners were sent to larger installations in the North so rapidly that only 328 men were handled in the following month.

An official inspection in late August found excellent conditions in the fort's hospital but labeled the prisoners' quarters "filthy" and "a disgrace to humanity and the service." The report recommended the immediate erection of two rough prison buildings with a combined capacity of 1,000 and a hospital capable of housing 50 to 100. By fall the two new prison buildings had been constructed next to the stable on the east side of the fort, and an addition to the hospital had been made near the gate.

Unfortunately, no photographs of the fort exist from this period, because, as the Baltimore *Sun* reported in October, 1863, the Provost Marshall of Baltimore "Colonel Fish . . . seized all the pictures in the various book stores of this city which represented the different fortifications, forts, . . . that the government does not wish to be too well known."

Life among the prisoners at this time was generally dull, punctuated only by meals—which were also dull—and such amusements as the prisoners could devise for themselves.

The meals? Breakfast was often coffee and hardtack. A second meal was usually *beans* and hardtack. The main meal may have featured a half-pound serving of salt pork or pickled beef. And hardtack. The few Southerners who could afford to bought fresh fruit and vegetables from sutlers, civilian "entrepeneurs" who set up small businesses inside the fort.

Fort McHenry 1865   *Maryland Historical Society*

Amusements consisted of rat hunts (these were necessities as much as diversions), ball games, debates on often-silly subjects, and mock parades which burlesqued the ceremonies conducted daily by the guards.

Still, prison was prison, and in the latter part of November, 1863, a group of Confederate surgeons who had been captured at Gettysburg, wrote to Colonel William Hoffman, Commissary General of Prisoners in Washington, to complain about the severe and unfair treatment they were receiving at Fort McHenry. Colonel Hoffman, on December 17, sent a copy of the letter to Colonel P. A. Porter, Commanding Officer at Fort McHenry, and demanded an immediate reply. The following excerpts are taken from Colonel Porter's reply, dated December 19:

> "The food has been good and well prepared, the coffee better than that used by several companies of the garrison. I acknowledge that water for bathing is not being furnished the prisoners. I found it necessary to refuse admittance to the lady visitors, as when admitted they acted in some instances upon the principle that 'All was fair in love and war', and disobeyed the rules of the post. The prisoners are allowed to go out upon a balcony for sun and air during the day, and go down into the prison yard for water roll-call. Some ninety Government blankets were distributed among them. Soft bread has been allowed to several who needed it. Some few have bedding. It was for the above, I suppose, that I am indebted to the surgeons' unfavorable diagnosis of my character, which has filled me with astonishment rather than any other sensation. Considering how our prisoners fared at Richmond their demands were rather extraordinary. I have replied, I believe, fully to the communications referred to me; not by mere answers to special allegations, but by the fullest information concerning the treatment of prisoners here. I do not claim that the prison arrangements are perfect, but I do claim that humanity has something to do with all the regulations of this post, and that I shall be thankful if the chance of war shall never subject me to greater hardships than are felt in prison life at Fort McHenry."

Statistics seem to bear out Colonel Porter's claim of humanity. Whereas death tolls at some Civil War prisons were staggering, fatalities at Fort McHenry totaled only 15. In addition, there were three executions. The victims were: Private Joseph Kuhne, 2nd Maryland Regiment, hanged on March 7, 1862, for the murder of an officer; Andrew Laypole, cavalryman under J.E.B. Stuart, hanged May 23, 1864, as a Confederate spy and guerilla; and George W. McDonald, 3rd Maryland Cavalry, charged with desertion and assault and shot by a firing squad on September 21, 1864.

Ironically, there may have been some deaths among the Federal guards. In a letter to his wife on October 16, 1864, Private George Washington Kimball, a carpenter (and the fort's gallows builder) with Comapny G of the 5th Massachusetts Volunteer Milita, wrote in part:

> "I expect to get 40 cent pr. day for all my time here. So I shant be as poor as you may think. I wish you had some of our good Peaches and Sweet Potatoes out here. They are very plenty. We got splendid peaches for 5 cts a qt. I dont buy anything for fear of getting poisened as two of the Regt have been poisened since we came in the fort. I have know doubt but what any of the Baltimoreiens would Kill us they dar to. They are a sower looking lot."

Despite the security measures, records acknowledge 38 escapes between March, 1863, and May, 1865. In the same period only 15 men died, a far cry from the heavy mortality records of many larger Union and Confederate prison camps. Following the Gettysburg influx, the monthly total of prisoners handled usually ranged between 250

Political Prisoners

Judge Richard G. Carmichael

Charles Howard
Police Commissioner of Baltimore

William Wilkens Glenn
Editor of Baltimore Exchange

Confederate POWs

Dr. William P. Young

Colonel Roger W. Hanson

Captain Victor Von Sheliha

Lieutenant William Jones

Colonel John Pegram

Captain Harry W. Gilmore

Union Soldiers

Colonel A. B. R. Sprague

Captain Barbour
Provost Marshall at the fort, 1864

Lieutenant Edward L. Porter

All Photographs from the Collection of Eric Davis

and 350. During the last months of the war, the number dwindled sharply. The final return, dated September 1865, listed only four.

At the end of the year, only a small detachment of troops was stationed at Fort McHenry to handle the routine maintenance.

If during the War of 1812 Fort McHenry entered the annals of military history, the Civil War saw it find a place in the development of Constitutional interpretation. The incidents in question revolved around one John Merryman, a citizen of Baltimore County and a Southern sympathizer who was arrested for treason on May 25, 1861.

Merryman had been implicated in the burning of railroad bridges around Baltimore (to prevent the passage of Union troops to Washington) on the night of April 19, 1861—but the case did not end with his arrest. His lawyer had sought a writ of habeus corpus (a writ that may be issued to bring a party before a court or judge, having as its function the release of a party from unlawful restraint) and had made application directly to Chief Justice Roger B. Taney.

When Merryman's case was called, United States Marshall Washington Bonifant reported that he had gone to Fort McHenry to serve the writ, but had been denied admittance. Taney proceeded to hold that Merryman's detention was unlawful on two grounds: "First—That the President, under the Constitution of the United States, cannot suspend the privilege of the writ of habeas corpus, nor authorize a military officer to do it. Second—a military officer has no right to arrest and detain a person not subject to the rule and articles of war for an offense against the laws of the United States, except in aid of the judicial authority and subject to its control."

To avoid any possible misunderstanding, the Chief Justice said he would put his opinion in writing for delivery directly to President Lincoln. He did so on Friday,

John Merryman   *Eric Davis*

June 1, in language as ringing as any to ever have been written in the long Anglo-American struggle for individual liberty. The heart of the matter was described thusly: "If the authority which the Constitution has confided to the judiciary department and judicial officers may thus upon any pretext or under any circumstances be usurped by the military power at its discretion, the people of the United States are no longer living under a government of laws, but every citizen holds life, liberty and property at the will and pleasure of the army officer in whose military district he may happen to be found."

Under other circumstances, the President probably would have supported Taney's views. Military necessity came first, however, and Lincoln opted to ignore the order and opinion. Nevertheless, the Administration was anxious to play the incident down. On July 4, 1861, Secretary of War Cameron interviewed Merryman at Fort McHenry, and on July 12, ordered that he be delivered to Bonifant, in tacit, albeit belated, compliance with Taney's order. Eventually, although Merryman was indicted for treason, he was released on bond and never brought to trial.

One hundred years later, in a court ceremony commemorating the anniversary of the case, formally known as *Ex Parte Merryman*, William L. Marbury of Baltimore discussed its continuing significance. "The role of Chief Justice Taney," he said, "symbolizes the deepest aspirations of our times. All of us must surely entertain the hope that the rule of law will ultimately replace the use of naked power. I realize that this is beginning to be a shopworn phrase. But just as the ordinary man may be confused by the debates of theologians and yet be moved by the examples of the saints, so . . . he may respond in his inmost being to a great act of faith, such as the ruling of Chief Justice Taney in the Merryman case. For in the last analysis, it is Taney's faith in the rule of law which breathes through the opinion in that case."

Justice Roger Brooke Taney   *Dan Toomey*

Civil War

Fort McHenry, Baltimore Bastille
The Civil War Years—1861–1865

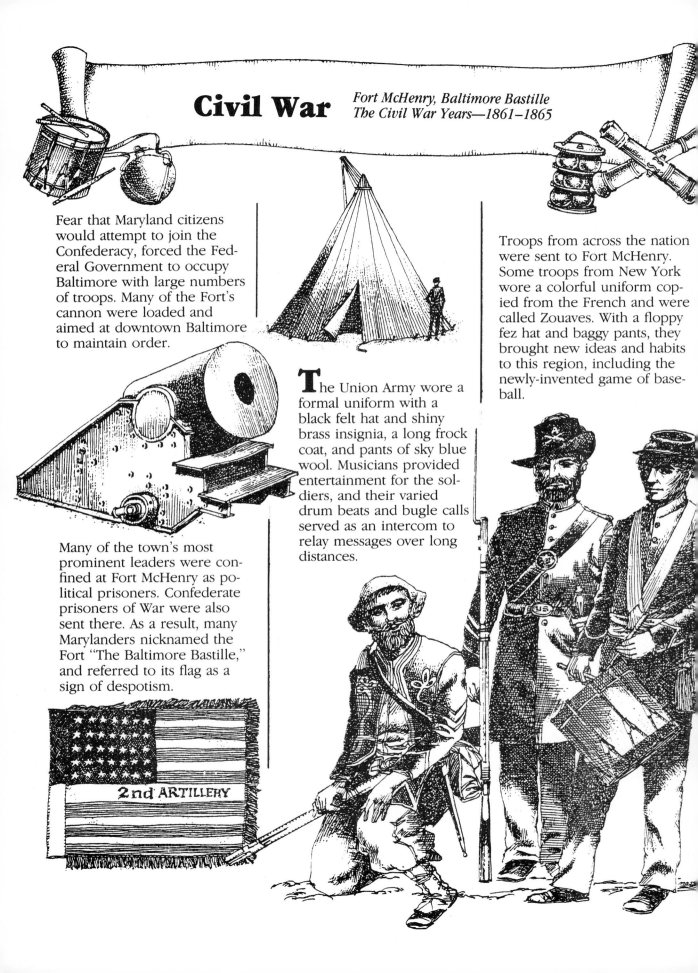

Fear that Maryland citizens would attempt to join the Confederacy, forced the Federal Government to occupy Baltimore with large numbers of troops. Many of the Fort's cannon were loaded and aimed at downtown Baltimore to maintain order.

Many of the town's most prominent leaders were confined at Fort McHenry as political prisoners. Confederate prisoners of War were also sent there. As a result, many Marylanders nicknamed the Fort "The Baltimore Bastille," and referred to its flag as a sign of despotism.

The Union Army wore a formal uniform with a black felt hat and shiny brass insignia, a long frock coat, and pants of sky blue wool. Musicians provided entertainment for the soldiers, and their varied drum beats and bugle calls served as an intercom to relay messages over long distances.

Troops from across the nation were sent to Fort McHenry. Some troops from New York wore a colorful uniform copied from the French and were called Zouaves. With a floppy fez hat and baggy pants, they brought new ideas and habits to this region, including the newly-invented game of baseball.

2nd ARTILLERY

A PAUSE AND THE CENTENNIAL

I N THE LAST DECADES of the 19th century and the early years of the 20th, Fort McHenry continued to be part of Baltimore City's life—first as a military garrison, then as a public park, still later, during the First World War, as a major military hospital.

After the Civil War it became customary to transfer the fort's officers frequently. Many of the garrison's enlisted men, however, remained on duty there for years. They married local women, established homes, and raised children in the nearby Locust Point neighborhood.

In 1877, when the Maryland National Guard was called out to quell a riotious railroad strike, the troops at Fort McHenry were put in readiness, at the request of state authorities, to join in restoring civil order. But the Guard succeeded in quieting the disturbances, so the principal peacetime function of the troops at Fort McHenry remained marching in street parades.

One of the biggest of those parades was held when Baltimore celebrated the seventy-fifth anniversary of "The Star-Spangled Banner." Eight war vessels re-enacted the bombardment of Fort McHenry. The display was so popular that similar re-enactments became almost annual events in later years.

For a long time it had been rumored that the War Department planned to abandon the fort as a military post and on one occasion Mayor Ferdinand C. Latrobe, ever on the lookout for park sites, had gone to Washington to tell President Ulysses S. Grant—rather bluntly—"We want Fort McHenry." Grant had merely smiled and replied, "I understand that during the Civil War some of your people wanted to *take* it."

But Fort McHenry remained open. Young beech trees, planted along the driveway just inside the gate, grew to handsome maturity. Baltimoreans visited to watch army mules work an amazing treadmill which sawed wood for the soldiers, and to gape at bugler Joseph Martini, famed as the only man to have escaped death at Custer's Last Stand. He had been sent with a message for reinforcements as Custer's troops moved up on the Little Bighorn, and so was happily absent during the massacre.

In 1872, the Corps of Engineers undertook the construction of a new water battery at Fort McHenry. The engineers located it northeast of the fort, near the sea wall, on approximately the same site where the lower water battery had stood during the War of 1812. The original plan for this massive earthen work called for the placement of 25 15-inch guns. By 1876 a parapet sufficiently large to cover ten guns, three traverse magazines and the platforms had been completed but later that year the

A Peaceful Afternoon in 1870 at the Fort

Army suspended all funding for the work. Two years later an engineer recommended that the battery be completed, but his plea fell on deaf ears. Again in 1892, the Baltimore district engineer also urged completion of the neglected battery and installation of modern guns. That the Army never resumed work on it was indicative of the declining importance of Fort McHenry as a coastal fortification.

As the end of the century approached, Baltimoreans realized their city lacked facilities to dry-dock the new, large vessels of the North German Lloyd and Allan Lines. The need was met by a group led by John W. Garrett and his two sons, Robert and T. Harrison Garrett, who organized the Baltimore Dry-Dock Company. With a shipyard as part of the project, it was decided that the site should include five acres of Fort McHenry, provided the land could be purchased from the government. A bill to that effect was passed by Congress in 1878, but it contained the proviso that in return for the land, government vessels could be docked there free of charge. In 1884,

Mock Bombardment During 75th Anniversary of the War of 1812

the dry dock and its adjuncts were leased by the Baltimore Dry-Dock Company to the Columbian Iron Works & Dry Dock Company. Within six years the Columbian Iron Works & Dry Dock Company ranked as one of the largest of its kind in the nation.

The only activity at Fort McHenry connected with the Spanish-American War (1889) was the drilling of Maryland National Guardsmen inducted into federal service.

Early in the new century, the flagstaff, then located on the east bastion, became the topic of much discussion. The post quartermaster first brought the subject up when he asked for $40 to paint it. Department headquarters turned him down because he had used the wrong account number!

Shortly thereafter, the fort's Captain Charles Gerhardt proposed the memorialization of the presumably still-unpainted flagstaff. The captain believed that the flagstaff was then located at the exact spot where it had been during the bombardment in 1814. In addition, he implied that Francis Scott Key had written "The Star-Spangled Banner" at the fort rather than in Baltimore. Consequently, Gerhardt recommended that "a bronze tablet be erected near the flagstaff giving on one half a short history of the event and the name of the author and on the other half, the song in full."

Interior of the Star Fort (circa 1890)   *Maryland Historical Society*

Major Medorem Crawford, the post commander, enthusiastically endorsed Gerhardt's letter, adding that large numbers of persons visited Fort McHenry annually because of its historical significance. The department commander then added his own thoughts: "A flagstaff as tall as possible and in proper proportion, should be erected on the very spot in question and from this a flag should fly at all times, day and night."

Gerhardt's letter made the rounds of the general staff in Washington—until it reached Brigadier General John Patton Story, Chief of Artillery. Story pointed out that Key had not written the anthem at Fort McHenry. More important, Story did some research on his own and was "not able to verify the statement of Captain Gerhardt that our flag is now displayed at the same point it was flying at the British bombardment." While one does not know what source Story had available to him, his problem can

Fourth Regiment, Maryland National Guard, on parade at the Fort in 1894   *Courtesy, The Baltimore Sun*

well be understood today. The only extant pre-1812 plan of the fort on which the flagstaff is shown indicates that it was in the corner of the parade ground where the replica now stands. The first postwar map to show the flagstaff located it in the bastion where it was when Gerhardt wrote his letter. Exactly when the Army moved it remains unknown. At any rate, although a new flagstaff was not acquired, a tablet dedicated to Francis Scott Key was installed at Fort McHenry by May 7, 1906.

That same year, Fort McHenry became faced with a governmental situation far more serious than the red tape which had prevented the flagstaff from getting a new coat of paint. During the fall, the Department of Agriculture asked permission to use the fort as a cattle quarantine. The Baltimore *News* of November 29, 1906, published the following report regarding the request:

> *"The Proposal to turn Fort McHenry over to the Bureau of Animal Industry for a 'cattle pen' is felt very keenly by Colonel Harry R. Anderson, commanding the artillery district of Baltimore. He has taken the matter up with Brigadier General Frederick D. Grant, who is in command of the Department of the East. So far he has received no answer to his recommendations on the subject. Orders for the abandonment of the Fort as an army post have been issued, but no announcement of its future has been officially made by the War Department. As is well known, the Bureau of Animal Industry the Department of Agriculture applied for permission to use it as a cattle quarantine station several months ago. Inspectors from the Bureau have visited the Post several times to examine it."*

At that time, Colonel Anderson sent a letter to General Grant, asking that the post be retained for tactical, strategic, and sentimental reasons. He noted that it was the base of supplies for the entire district and called special attention both to its splendid location on a deep-water channel and to the presence of a railroad terminal right outside its gate. The facts that the supplies for all the local posts were sent through Fort McHenry and that government boats landed at the small pier from six to a dozen times a day were also presented.

Colonel Anderson, in talking of the danger of the fort being turned over the the Bureau of Animal Industry, said: "Orders for the abandonment of the Fort have already been issued. They do not say that Fort McHenry will be abandoned, but if carried out they will mean the complete evacuation of the post. If the post is given up there will be no one there to look after things, the flag could not be kept floating over the old ramparts. As commander of the district, I will do all in my power to preserve the famous old fort."

But the Army proceeded with its plans and announced that the fort would be abandoned on March 31, 1907. With that deadline in mind, the post quartermaster ceased to make any but emergency repairs to the structures of the post. Then, on March 20, it was learned that Fort McHenry was not to be abandoned after all. The strength of the post at that time consisted of only one officer and fewer than 15 enlisted men. This skeleton force remained from April, 1906, to May, 1907, when a battery from the 141st Coast Artillery arrived for duty.

Fort McHenry was to continue as an active post for five more years. Then, on July 13, 1912, a telegram arrived announcing the end of more than a century of military history. Following a communication from the War Department dated July 12, the telegram repeated:

"Issue orders relieving 141st Company—from duty at Fort McHenry—to Fort Strong, Mass. for station. Fort McHenry will be turned over to caretakers to be furnished by

Guarding the Entrance to Force McHenry, 1900

National Park Service, Fort McHenry

Quartermaster's Department."

On July 21, 1912, the day after the troops left Fort McHenry, this item appeared in the Baltimore *Sun*:

> *"The sunset gun roared dismally out on the rain swept Patapsco last night as the flag, which the British could not shoot away, was hauled down by a lone soldier. No bugle blast sounded retreat; no soldiers stood with bared heads. Fort McHenry was dead.*
>
> *"At 7 o'clock in the evening, 20 minutes before the flag came down, the One Hundred and Forty-first Company of Coast Artillery marched out through the old gate. The sentries, who for over a century have paced the flagstones there, fell in behind.*
>
> *"The iron barriers, which had seldom been used, because a soldier with a musket proved a better guard, clicked together on rusted hinges and an oldtime padlock clasped them together. Inside the great rolling acres, where men of the flag have trod for many years, there were but four soldiers left. Tomorrow even they will be gone.*
>
> *"When night came the old fort lay wrapped in gloom and mist. Where once the light of company rooms had flashed yellow against the dusk and glint of a soldiers bayonet shone in the dark were only eerie shadows of old guns that could not shoot.*
>
> *"Finally, at 6:30 o'clock the bugler sounded 'assembly' and with farewells the men hastily buckled on cartridge belts, shouldered their guns and fell into line. Some were missing at first, but they were routed out of corners, where girls had made them forget the bugle call, and ran into line.*
>
> *"Then came the order, 'March!' More than 1,000 persons were there to see the men leave and there was none who did not thrill at the call. The men looked*

Firing of the Rodman Cannons for the last time, July 4, 1904   *National Park Service, Fort McHenry*

FORT McHENRY

1776
WHETSTONE POINT
SHORE BATTERY

1794
STAR FORT BEGUN
LATER NAMED FOR
WASHINGTON'S
SECRETARY OF WAR

1795
RESERVATION PARTLY
ACQUIRED BY THE
UNITED STATES

1814
GALLANT DEFENCE
DURING BRITISH
BOMBARDMENT
INSPIRED THE
WRITING OF
"THE
STAR-SPANGLED
BANNER"

1838
FULL RESERVATION
CEDED

1914
TRANSFERRED TO THE CITY OF BALTIMORE
FOR USE AS A PUBLIC PARK

ERECTED BY THE MARYLAND DAUGHTERS OF THE AMERICAN REVOLUTION 1914

Dedication as a Baltimore City Park

Enoch Pratt Free Library

around the fort, the old buildings taking on new shapes in the growing dark. Then every person in the fort—soldier, civilian and women—looked up, where in the gloom the flag hung limply.

"There was no band to play. The crunch of the men's heels on the gravel walks was the only sound as they headed for the gate. There stood the last sentry which Fort McHenry probably will ever have. Down through the years has come his call 'Who goes there?'

"As he saw the troop swinging toward him, he shouldered his rifle and stepped to one side. As the last man swung out he wheeled and joined him and there was no sentry to speak out that thrilling call. At noon the caretaker, probably a retired enlisted man, with his walking stick, will sit at the gate basking in the sun.

"After the troops had embarked on the train, the last kiss had been stolen, the last baby kissed, a little lame girl, related to Corporal Stewart, stood out beyond the crowd. She could not come to the train after Stewart had kissed her she stood there crying until the light on the train had vanished.

"Lieutenant Payne, who until tomorrow will have charge of the fort, said that he will lock the gate today, because there will not be sufficient men to guard the property. After the War Department has appointed a caretaker for the fort, he says the gate will be reopened.

"The flag will still fly on the same staff where it flew on September 13, 1814, *when the British bombarded the fort, and until Monday, at least, the sunset gun will boom its salute. After that the gun will be silenced.*

"There is one person in the fort who was anxious about whether the flag would fly when the troops had gone. George Thomas, 5 years old and son of Electrical Sergeant Thomas, has planted a pole in front of his father's quarters and a tiny flag flies there.

" 'If nobody else does it,' said George yesterday, 'I'll see that my flag still flies. I know all about Francis Scott Key.' "

Nearly two years after the youthful gesture of patriotism, the city of Baltimore got what it had wanted since the days of Ulysses Grant: on May 21, 1914, Congress passed a bill leasing Fort McHenry to the city for use as a municipal park. The formal transfer took place June 27, when Congressman J. Charles Linthicum, acting for the Secretary of War, presented the lease to Mayor James H. Preston.

On September 7, the National Star-Spangled Banner Centennial was held in Baltimore. Week-long festivities began with the arrival of the U.S.S. *Constellation,* accompanied by a fleet of warships representing each type in the Navy, from the old frigate herself to the modern super-dreadnaught *Texas.* The *Constellation,* the oldest vessel in active service in the U.S. Navy, had been launched in Baltimore on that same date 117 years before.

The remaining days of the festival were filled with parades, athletic events, concerts, receptions, and military balls. The highlight of the centennial occurred on September 12, when a monument to Lieutenant Colonel George Armistead was unveiled on the outer battery at Fort McHenry. As 6,500 school children sang "The Star-Spangled Banner," Edward Berge, the sculptor, and George Armistead, Jr., a descendant of the defender, pulled a cord and an American flag fell to reveal the statue. By that time, the school children had formed a human flag, and from a distance the effect was startling. Each child was gowned and hooded with the proper color, and each had a matching handkerchief, which, when waved all together, gave the impression that the "flag" was actually fluttering in the breeze.

The Armistead monument is a bronze portrait figure which stood on the southeast salient of the outer work. It was erected by the Star-Spangled Banner Association and the Maryland Society of the War of 1812. (It remained on the outer battery until 1966 when it was moved to a position in front of the Visitor's Center, overlooking the harbor, across from Lazaretto.) At the same time, the ground was broken for the $75,000 national monument to Francis Scott Key. The Key monument was not completed and unveiled until 1922, as the growing threat of World War I imposed other priorities.

The next year, June 1, 1915, the City of Baltimore opened a new bathing beach and swimming pool at its new park. The facility immediately became a mecca for thousands of men, women, and children from all sections of the city and from the suburbs as well. For five cents they could have an afternoon of real enjoyment.

For the month of July there was an average daily attendance of more than 1,000 people, but on Sunday, July 4, there was a real onslaught, and the park's superintendent, Captain George W. Butterworth, was forced to close the gates at 4 P.M. By that time over 3,600 people had paid for lockers and bathing suits.

The pool was 200 by 300 feet with a bottom that gradually sloped to six feet. In the center of the pool was a diving raft which was the most attractive spot for the children.

Not only did the beach demonstrate that such a place was needed; it clearly

The Human Flag, September 12, 1914

The Flag House

indicated that mixed bathing was a success. Mixed bathing, it had been feared, would be a failure, and several other swimming pools in the city had not attempted it because officials were afraid it would meet with unfavorable reaction. When plans had been completed for the beach at Fort McHenry, however, the Public Bath Commission decided to risk mixed bathing—that is, to allow both sexes to splash around in the water at the same time. The commission's plans were criticized somewhat in the beginning, but, not many days after the opening, the experiment was deemed a success. Of course, one concession to lingering Victorian discretion had been made: whereas males and females were indeed allowed to bathe in the same water at the same time, they were separated by a rope! But, times being what they were, the rope quickly vanished.

Defenders' Day Bombardment

A. Aubrey Bodine

WORLD WAR I : THE HOSPITAL

THE RESORT-LIKE atmosphere of the fort-turned-park was shattered in 1917, when the military returned to build the United States Army General Hospital No. 2, a receiving hospital through which more than 20,000 wounded soldiers from World War I would pass for treatment on their way back to duty or to civilian life.

The project was originally started as a temporary hospital in August, 1917, under the command of Colonel Harry Selby Purnell, a regular Army medical officer. With him were 50 men of the Medical Corps from Forts Slocum and Wadsworth, New York, and Fort Howard, Maryland. The hospital involved the construction of 16 buildings, one psychiatric ward, one receiving ward, one nurses' home, and one mess and kitchen, all one-story structures. An addition or extension was authorized later which included: 23 two-story ward buildings, a two-story officers' quarters, two two-story nurses' quarters and two two-story school buildings.

Captain Maurice A. Hockman, Q.M.C., U.S.A., was assigned as constructing quartermaster on December 19, 1917. He reported to the site the next day, immediately took charge, and began to organize the field forces necessary to carry on the work. The contract had previously been let from the Washington Office to the J. Henry Miller Co., Inc., of Baltimore, and company representatives were on the grounds when Captain Hockman arrived. Actual work was started within 24 hours, and soon a full contingent of laborers, mechanics, and office staff was in full swing.

The impact of this extensive construction could have been disastrous to the historic structures had it not been for the alertness of the construction quartermaster officer. He wrote in his completion report:

> *"During the construction work of this project all the above ground historical landmarks have been religiously respected, and the General Hospital No. 2 has been built entirely around the original Fort and its landmarks without any encroachment, so that should it ever be deemed to raze the present hospital buildings, Fort McHenry will remain intact as one of the landmarks of American history."*

The quartermaster was as good as his word. All the historic structures within and without the old fort emerged from this experience virtually unscathed.

When the terrible flood of American war wounded began to flow back to the States, General Hospital No. 2 was ready. It was the largest receiving hospital in the country, and all types checked through it, with some remaining for treatment and some moving on to other hospitals.

The capacity of the hospital quickly grew to roughly 3,000 patients. The staff

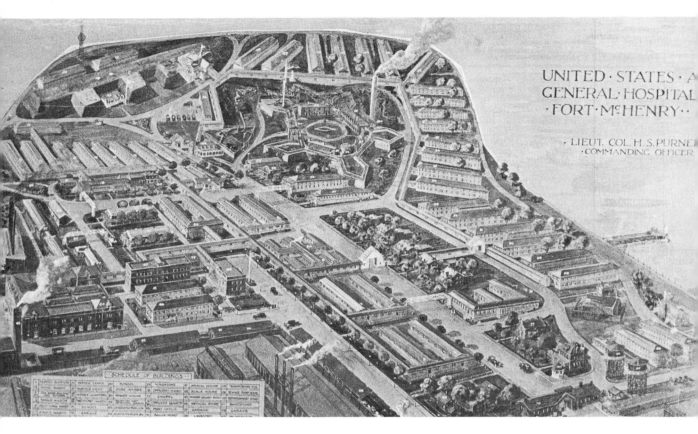

Bird's Eye View of General Hospital No. 2, Fort McHenry   *National Park Service, Fort McHenry*

Colonel Harry Purnell, Commander of U.S. General Hospital No. 2, at Fort McHenry
National Park Service, Fort McHenry

Hospital Nurses   *Enoch Pratt Free Library (Emily Raine Williams)*

included 200 doctors, 300 nurses, 100 civilian hospital aides, and 300 medical corpsmen. In addition to staff were friends and relatives of returning soldiers, who came to Baltimore from all over the country to see and comfort their loved ones while they were at the hospital.

As time moved along, Fort McHenry became less a receiving hospital and more a surgical center. Much medical history was made there, particularly in neuro-surgery. Advances were also made in plastic surgery. Soldiers who had lost portions of their faces left the hospital with new noses, new ears, and other seemingly miraculous results of the then-new surgical techniques.

Great strides were also made in occupational therapy. Lieutenant Walter Vanaman, of Baltimore, started the country's first school for disabled soldiers with equipment he borrowed from the Signal Corps. Many of the disabled men whom he taught telegraphy later obtained jobs in communication fields. News of the success of Vanaman's school finally reached Washington, and, after a comprehensive plan had been outlined by the government for vocational and therapeutic work, a school of telegraphy was established at each hospital.

Other subjects taught at Fort McHenry's vocational school were knitting, basketry, metal work, commercial art, shorthand, and typing. Carpentry, upholstery,

Pharmaceutical Lab at the Hospital   *National Park Service, Fort McHenry*

"The Troublebuster"
National Park Service, Fort McHenry

auto repair, and bookkeeping were also offered to keep the wounded occupied and provide them with a means of livelihood.

Probably the spirit of the whole rehabilitation program was depicted better than it could possibly have been done otherwise in a picture: the cover illustration on the anniversary number of "The Trouble Buster," Fort McHenry's own magazine, printed on its own presses by its own wounded men. The cover picture was of The Trouble Buster himself—a big, husky doughboy with his head swathed in bandages, a baseball bat in his hands, and one eye winking gleefully out upon the world, as though he were saying, "Come on! Pitch me the best you've got, because I'm going to smash it for a homer—wounds or no wounds."

Lieutenant Vanaman's innovations were not limited to the field of physical therapy. He was probably America's first disc jockey without even knowing it. Dances were held often at the hospital, and Lieutenant Vanaman provided the music for them by setting up a ten-watt transmitter beside a phonograph in one of the offices. This music was beamed to the Red Cross Hall, some 400 feet away, where it was picked up by a receiving set and amplified. There were no commercial broadcasting stations crowding the airways at that time, and on at least one occasion Lieutenant Vanaman's broadcast reached Hagerstown. It was picked up by a radio enthusiast while he and a friend were exchanging Morse signals on tiny crystal sets.

One of the most popular places at the fort during the six years it served as a hospital was its ivy-covered chapel. Thousands of wounded soldiers visited the chapel for a few moments of meditation and to give thanks for their safe return.

A one-story brick building, 27 by 55 feet, the chapel had been built in November, 1879, at a cost of $1,350. It contained a small vestibule, a vestry, and a 25-by-40-foot sanctuary which had a seating capacity of 120.

It had originally been intended for use as a chapel and a schoolhouse, but a report dated August, 1883, declared: "School not a success. The children go into Baltimore to school and the enlisted men won't attend unless compelled to."

The roots of the ivy which covered the chapel were originally brought from

Chapel 1890   *National Archives*

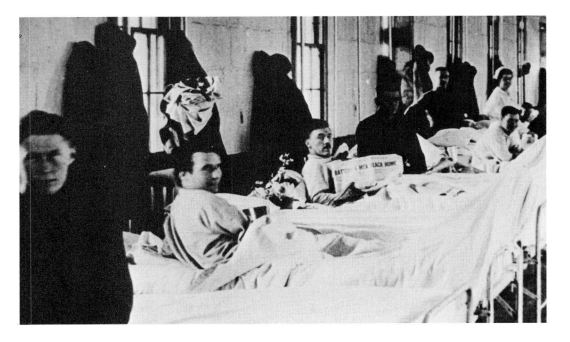

Recuperating Defenders in Hospital Ward   *National Park Service, Fort McHenry*

Abbotsford, Scotland, the home of Sir Walter Scott, by Washington Irving. They had been planted in the White House grounds in Washington. Some time in 1883, a number of the roots were obtained from the White House and planted around the chapel at the fort.

Chaplain Perry Wilcox tried to make the religious phase of life at Fort McHenry as strong and valuable as possible. He left no stone unturned to provide the very best service for the men of every faith. A Roman Catholic mass was held at 7 A.M. every Sunday morning, followed by an 11 A.M. service for Protestants. Every Friday at 7:30 P.M. there was a Jewish service, and on Sunday nights there was a Methodist singing service. Occasionally the quaint little chapel was the scene of military weddings. For some unexplained reason it was torn down in the summer of 1928.

An epidemic of flu took a heavy toll at the hospital in 1919, as it had done earlier throughout the rest of the country. Some 300 of the patients came down with it, and 100 of them died. The staff did not know much about flu virus then. They merely did the best they could, making the rounds of all the patients four times daily, sponging their faces and giving cool drinks of milk or orange juice.

On March 31, 1919, the War Department made public figures showing the number of patients in the various military hospitals. At that time, the facility at Fort McHenry was handling more patients than any other Army hospital in the United States. The number on that date at Fort McHenry was 2,109. Second on the list was General Hospital No. 28, at Fort Sheridan, Illinois, where there were 2,072 patients.

The bright side of all the hard work at Fort McHenry shows in some of the real sayings that went the rounds:

New patient to O.D. (who is taking his history): "In civil life I was an undertaker."

O.D.: "I thought you told me you were a physician."

New Patient: "You misunderstood me. I said I followed the medical profession."

The one story that everyone stationed at Fort McHenry really enjoyed was told of Major Jones' wife. When asked where Fort McHenry was, she replied, "At the end of the third smell." She was right, for the first was the guano plant, the second was the sugar refinery, and the third was the fertilizer factory at Curtis Bay.

The heavy traffic of wounded began tapering off toward the end of 1919, as other Army hospitals began sharing some of the burden. By 1920, the days of General Hospital No. 2 were numbered as patients were admitted to permanent hospitals. On May 31, 1920, the War Department closed the hospital and the reservation was transferred to the Public Health Service for use as a veterans' hospital.

One of the hardest-working "volunteers" at Fort McHenry during its hospital days was Jeff, a cross-bred Merino ram, who bled for his country for three and a half years. During the term of his service he gave an average of two ounces of blood a week to create certain laboratory media used to test patients' blood. The old ram contributed to more than 3,000 Wasserman tests, in which sheep's blood was indispensible.

Jeff entered the service in September, 1919, at the United States Public Service Hospital in Danville, New York. A year later he was transferred to Fort McHenry.

In February, 1923, he was retired, apparently worn out. But after five months' rest, Jeff began to recuperate from the loss of blood and to prove to the hospital attendants the error of the saying, "They never come back." In fact, he became so energetic he had to be shackled.

More than one hospital attendant, attempting to cross the enclosure in which Jeff and his successor, a stalwart young Southdown ram named Mutt, were kept, got driven over the nearest fence. At least six were butted when and where they least expected it. One day, Jeff escaped from his guards and took the recreation hall by storm. Visitors, nurses, convalescing patients and soldiers promptly sought refuge on billiard tables and other elevated places where Jeff's hard head could not reach them.

After the disturbance, Major Howard W. Barker, commandant of the hospital, announced that he would only call on Jeff in an emergency, but that he would use him to train the young successor, Mutt. Training was something Mutt sorely needed. Many times, before he was put in the enclosure with Jeff, the newcomer had led the laboratory men a hot chase over the hospital grounds. Soon, however, the two animals became inseparable, and, since Jeff was hobbled, Mutt was easily caught when wanted.

In the fall of 1923, with the hospital closing down, Jeff was sent to a farm in Baltimore County, where he spent his remaining days chasing the farmer's ewes.

Mutt, disconsolate at the loss of his companion, became moody and irritable. After vainly attempting to comfort him, the hospital authorities ordered his removal to a hospital in Washington. The weary attendants who tried to hold him said a silent prayer for the safety of the capital.

On June 14, 1922, 15,000 people—the truly patriotic and the merely curious as well—crammed into Fort McHenry to hear President Warren G. Harding deliver an address at the unveiling of a memoral to Francis Scott Key.

As the presidential motorcade entered the fort, it passed through a line of sentries in olive drab, who snapped to salute with fixed bayonets as President Harding passed. Within a few moments they were face to face with the human tragedies of the Great War: the "young defenders," maimed and weary, bandaged of body and limb,

Fort McHenry's Baseball Team 1919

National Park Service, Fort McHenry

huddling in wheel chairs with nurses in white all around them.

There the President of the United States halted. He let the crowd in the big stand before the monument wait. He let the reception committee in their tall hats and taller dignity wait. He let *everything* wait while he talked to the doughboys who had seen "by the dawn's early light" things that had inspired no anthems, but had, instead, torn their souls and bodies.

They had been proud men when they had boarded their transports to fight overseas for the flag. Their spirits were still high, but their bodies were broken, and they were being nursed back to health at the Fort McHenry Hospital. Unflinching in the field, they were as shy as bashful schoolgirls when President Harding greeted them—yet their eyes shone even as their lips faltered.

Down the long line of wheel chairs walked the President, giving a smile, a firm handshake, or a word of cheer to each of the veterans. Following closely was Mrs. Harding with an attendant, who distributed carnations and red roses.

"How do you do?" "I'm very glad to meet you." "How are you getting along?" "I'm awfully glad to see you." Those warm, friendly words were the President's most frequent greetings.

At the end of the line of invalids' chairs was a slim, emaciated figure. His voice scarcely was audible when he attempted to return the President's salutation. President Harding took his hand and held it long. "You'll be better soon," the President said as he gazed into the eyes of the veteran, little more than a boy. And then he added, "I sincerely hope so."

Then through the hospital he went, shaking hands with at least 300 patients and members of the hospital staff. His voice was always modulated, his smile always apparent. There was no somberness in his demeanor; his message was ever one of cheer.

After greeting the last patient, the President joined the great crowd around the flag-veiled monument, where General Pershing's own band from Fort Hunt was exhausting its stock of tunes, and the on-lookers were twisting their necks trying to spot the President.

As Harding came into view and the band played "Hail to the Chief," the crowd arose and cheered. The official ceremonies had begun. J. Cookman Boyd, president of the Park Board, introduced Lieutenant Colonel Clarence O. Sherrill, personal representative of the Secretary of War, and John Wingate Weeks, chairman of the dedication exercises. After a few brief remarks Lieutenant Colonel Sherrill introduced Bishop John Gardner Murray, who delivered the invocation.

As soon as Colonel Sherrill announced that the unveiling would take place, Miss Katherine Ethel Broening, daughter of the Mayor of Baltimore, and Miss Marie J. Neihaus, daughter of the sculptor Charles J. Neihaus, walked toward the base of the monument. They were dressed in white and carried bouquets of pink roses. The cords were put into their hands, they pulled, and two flags parted, revealing an immense bronze figure of Orpheus, god of music, standing on a white marble pedestal. A profile of Francis Scott Key was engraved in the marble base, and the words "To Francis Scott Key author of the Star-Spangled Banner and to the soldiers and sailors who took part in the Battle of North Point and the Defense of Fort McHenry in the War of 1812." As the flags swung away and the figure stood clear, a chorus of high school girls sang "The Star-Spangled Banner."

At the conclusion of a speech by J. Mayhew Wainwright, Assistant Secretary of War, Colonel Sherrill presented Mr. Neihaus, whom the Colonel hailed as one of the foremost sculptors in the world, yet a man simple in habit, modest in demeanor,

Soldiers arrive at the Fort, 1918

and gentle of manner. Mr. Neihaus stepped forward and forthwith proved the Colonel's assessment of his personality to be an accurate one. He acknowledged his introduction with a courteous bow, but he uttered not a word.

President Harding then prepared to make the concluding address. As Colonel Sherrill presented him to the audience, a sprinkle of rain fell, and there was a general raising of umbrellas and donning of raincoats and hats, for there were indications of a downpour. "Let me say at the outset," said President harding, "that I will take it as no discourtesy to the President if any of you seek shelter while I am speaking. I am a Baptist and don't care how hard it rains."

After the President made a number of extemporaneous remarks in which he praised the city of Baltimore and its people, he read the speech which he had prepared for the occasion. The highlight occurred when he said:

> *"One need not tell a Maryland audience how significant was the failure of the night attack on Fort McHenry. It spelled the failure of the most ambitious project ever put forth for the subjugation of this continent. The Maryland Militia and the limited force of regulars saved the Chesapeake, and won for Baltimore the distinction of being the only great seaport on the Atlantic coast which has never been occupied by an enemy. I trust that for all the future, Baltimore will have to share that fortune with every other seaport; but the fact remains that when the British armada of 1814 retired, beaten, from Fort McHenry, it left with Baltimore the eminence of being the one great American port over which no enemy flag has ever waved."*

While the President spoke, a wreath of white carnations and red roses, with flags of the War Mothers and Service Star Legion, lay against the monument's base, and the replica of the old flag of Fort McHenry, hauled to the top of the pole by Major Herman Reiss, a veteran of the fort's garrison, flapped gently in the harbor breeze.

By the fall of 1922, arrangements were already well along for transferring the remaining patients to permanent hospitals. The last patients to leave the Fort McHenry Hospital were Lieutenant Wingate Smith, and Privates John E. Alverson, James J. Plunkett, and John M. Little. On October 31, 1923, they were transferred to the University Hospital, where they were placed in contract beds. For the first time in the six years a hospital had been there, not a veteran was in the Fort McHenry institution for treatment.

World War I

U.S. General Hospital No. 2, Fort McHenry
Caring for the Wounded—1918–1925

By the beginning of the First World War, Baltimore had grown so large that Fort McHenry was no longer of strategic military importance.

The 40 acres of ground surrounding the old brick Fort had easy access to ships returning from France. Construction covered almost every inch of ground and provided an excellent location for a hospital.

Many nurses were employed by the Army. Dressed in starched white aprons and caps, their skills and caring helped thousands to a speedy recovery. Army doctors, working with local medical schools, developed many new surgical techniques.

The last of the patients was released in 1925, and the hospital buildings were torn down. The old brick Fort and its silent cannon were all that remained of 125 years of military occupation.

Many of the soldiers fighting in the trenches suffered from facial wounds. The newly equipped hospital pioneered in facial reconstruction and physical rehabilitation, and taught the men new job skills.

McHENRY, A NATIONAL PARK

ON JANUARY 4, 1924, Maryland Congressman J. Charles Linthicum, the same gentleman who worked so diligently to have "The Star-Spangled Banner" proclaimed our national anthem, introduced a bill to make Fort McHenry a national park. When the bill passed the House of Representatives, the Maryland Congressional delegation called on Secretary of War Weeks on February 18, 1925, and succeeded in enlisting his support. A few days later the bill was passed by the U. S. Senate and was signed by President Calvin Coolidge, March 3, 1925. The new law designated the reservation as Fort McHenry National Park and placed it under the administration of the United States Army.

The transfer of jurisdiction over the area was effected speedily, smoothly, and without incidents, but a frustrating situation confronted the Army in its effort to carry out the restoration. It was the same old song: funds were not immediately available. However, the dilapidated condition of the fort and the "forlorn and dismal" appearance of the area were creating so much hostile comment that Colonel Theodore W. Hacker, quartermaster of the Third Corps Area, was alloted $6,000 to hire temporary laborers to clean up the grounds. In October, 1925, he announced that, for the present at least, the work would consist of the "cultivation of plants, trees and shrubbery already in the ground and the addition of others."

In the same month, Colonel Hacker accepted an offer of $28,522.35 for the surplus buildings. The contractor agreed to dismantle and remove the buildings from the area, fill and grade the resultant excavations, and remove the rubble from the grounds. The Baltimore *Sun* reported on September 5, 1926, that all the buildings had been removed.

Although the area was now clean and funds were available, the Army still failed to initiate its program. For the balance of the year nothing was accomplished apart from some minor maintenance work, destruction of weeds, and removal of litter. The major cause for the delay was, without doubt, the difficulty encountered by the quartermaster in the formulation of his restoration plan. The inactivity led to severe criticism and presented a public relations problem which plagued the military.

In 1931, to further enhance the attractions offered by Fort McHenry as "restored" by the Army, the Daughters of the American Revolution planted a cutting from the elm tree beneath which Washington is said to have assumed command of the Continental Army at Cambridge, Massachusetts, July 3, 1775.

The cutting, surrounded by an iron railing, was planted at one side of the main driveway near the entrance to the old star fort. A tablet was affixed to the fence

Orpheus—Greek Muse of Poetry and Music

National Park Service, Fort McHenry

"Old Canteen in Motion" 1925

Courtesy, *The Baltimore Sun*

bearing the D.A.R. insignia with the explanation that:

"The Maryland State Society of the Daughters of the American Revolution planted this tree in commemoration of the Two Hundredth Anniversary of the Birth of George Washington 1732–1932."

In addition, 48 small red oak trees were planted along the walkway between Fort Avenue and the entrance to the fort. Each tree represented one of the United States, and each was designated by a state marker showing the date when that state was admitted to the Union.

At the same time, 30 cherry trees were planted by Baltimore City school children along the walkway to the Francis Scott Key Monument. Each tree was designated by a marker and dedicated to a hero of the battle of September 13 and 14, 1814. Each marker was sponsored by a local organization. The dedication of both sets of trees was held on September 12, 1932.

In time, still others were to follow the example set by the Daughters of the American Revolution. In 1936, the National Society of the Daughters of 1812 gave a collection of replicas of old furniture of the type which could have been used in the commanding officer's headquarters; then, in 1935, the E. Berkley Bowie Collection of weapons, consisting of 400 pieces, was donated to the fort by the Maryland Society of 1812.

Although it was believed in Baltimore that the Army would commence work in December, 1926, it was not until the spring of the following year that the quartermaster embarked on a very modest restoration program. The bulk of funds secured from the

A Young Patriot Views "forlorn and dismal" Star Fort 1925   *Courtesy The Baltimore Sun*

salvage operation was quickly expended on three items: the reinstallation of the entire electrical system, the addition of a second story to the junior officers' quarters, and renovation of the caretaker's quarters. In August the program came to a halt when the balance of the money was spent cleaning the buildings, reconditioning the commandant's quarters, and repairing the roofs.

The limited project evoked a flood of protest climaxed by a letter from William Norris, president of the Baltimore Park Board, to the authorities. In it he condemned the appearance of the fort as "a national disgrace."

Toward the end of the 1920s, the Army began to restore the fort in earnest—but the first step the military took was anything but restoration. General William E. Horton, Quartermaster Corps, wrote the Adjutant General in December, 1928, requesting authority to remove the partly-completed water battery dating from 1873. He gave three reasons for its removal: it was not associated with the War of 1812, it obstructed the view of the harbor, and he needed its material elsewhere. The Army approved and the battery disappeared.

Lieutenant Clifford Smith, construction quartermaster at Fort Meade, Maryland, took charge of the restoration work. He was later transferred to Puerto Rico, and Captain H. N. Williams then took over in April of 1928 and saw the work to its completion. At last the old barracks within the fort corresponded to their appearance in the late 1830s. (At the time of the restoration, the most completely documented information on the fort was from that period.)

In 1933, Fort McHenry National Park (the designation of which was changed in 1939 to National Monument and Historic Shrine) was transferred from the Army to the National Park Service, Department of the Interior, with the unusual stipulation that: "The Secretary of War may, in case of a national emergency, close the said Fort McHenry and use it for any and all military purposes during the period of the emergency." In conformity with this provision, the historic fort did indeed perform limited service during World War II, when part of it was assigned temporarily to the Navy for use as a fire-control school.

By an official proclamation on July 3, 1948, President Harry Truman authorized the display of the American flag "at all times during day and night" at Fort McHenry, thereby giving full legality to a custom which had been in effect at the fort since January 31, 1947.

Acting under authority of a 1942 law permitting him to modify the universal custom of displaying the flag from sunrise to sunset, the President declared that the flag should be flown at all times at the fort "as a perpetual symbol of our patriotism." Although the presidental proclamation stated that the flag would be flown "except when the weather is inclement," the officials at the fort decided that the policy of keeping "Old Glory" flying at all times, come storm or fair weather, would be continued.

At that time, at only one other place, on the Capitol at Washington, did the flag fly 24 hours each day on property owned or administered by the United States Government. However, the same custom prevailed at at least two other sites—one at Frederick, Maryland, at the grave of Francis Scott Key, and the other in Worcester, Massachusetts.

1926 aerial of the Fort, removing the hospital buildings *National Park Service, Fort McHenry*

Baltimoreans Celebrate at Fort McHenry 1931

In Frederick, according to local authorities, the flag, "flies by custom and not specific permission." In Worcester, when the War Memorial was designed, it was planned around the idea that the flag would fly perpetually, and it has flown there, night and day, since the building was dedicated on November 11, 1933.

Nowhere, however, does the practice have more significance than it has at Fort McHenry, where the banner's stars and stripes, always aloft, forever remind Americans of their proud heritage.

HISTORIC RAISINGS
AND THE TAVERN

IN 1956 THE NATIONAL PARK SERVICE began a ten-year project called Mission 66. The goals at Fort McHenry were to conduct historical and archaeological research, to build a visitors' center, develop a film dramatizing the bombardment and the writing of "The Star-Spangled Banner," and to improve services and provide programs to park visitors. Researchers gathered historical information from such facilities as the National Archives, the Baltimore City Archives, the Maryland Historical Society, and the Library of Congress. The HARP (Historical and Archaeological Research Project) Library at the fort was established in 1964 to house this information.

In 1958 the first controlled archaeological expedition at the fort was conducted under the guidance of G. Hubert Smith, National Park Service archaeologist. On September 12 of that year, 144 years after the historic British shelling, the Department of the Interior announced that the site of the fort's 1814 flag pole had been discovered. During the archaeological excavations, the research team had uncovered the massive hand-hewn oak timbers which had formed the supporting brace or step at the base of the pole. The timbers were found seven feet in the mud beneath the parade ground, where they had been well-preserved by ground water. After undergoing conservation procedures, the historic timbers were put on exhibition in the visitors' center.

A new 87-foot wooden staff was erected on the exact site of the original in time for the first official raising of the United States' new 49-star flag. Construction of the new pole was made possible by funds donated by the New York Community Trust.

The pole, an accurate reproduction of the original, was made by George J. Pultz, a steeplejack and president of the Flagpole and Equipment Company of Upper Marlboro, Maryland. The steeplejack spent months drawing flagstaff blueprints to government specifications and sawing, honing, and smoothing four logs of laminated Douglas fir. Unlike the original staff, which was supported by two nine-foot, hand-hewn oak timbers, the new pole is held by a steel sleeve embedded in ten feet of concrete.

At one minute after midnight on July 4, 1959, the 49-star flag was raised for the first time at Fort McHenry. The Baltimore *Sun* on July 4, 1959, reported: "The Secretary of the Interior, Fred A. Seaton, representing President Dwight D. Eisenhower, manned the halyards as the nation's new emblem was unfurled over the site of its most proudly hailed triumph. To the strains of the national anthem, in the glare of a battery of spotlights, the new flag of the United States—now 49 strong with the addition of

Pewter Mug Signed by the Defenders of Fort McHenry   *Maryland Historical Society*

Alaska—broke at the top of the new pole.

"The following message from President Eisenhower was read by Secretary Seaton to the throng of 30,000 clustered inside and on the fort's ramparts:

" *'The knowledge of a growing America fills us with pride, but we know too that our growing strength has brought new responsibilities. As a nation we are today responsible for the rights and liberties of twenty times as many Americans as once lived under the protecting guns of Fort McHenry.*

" *'And as a leader among the nations, we bear major responsibility for the mutual security of the free world. Our independence, therefore, is no longer celebrated alone. Our friends and allies join with us on this happy occasion. We in turn declare anew our responsibility for helping to advance the cause of freedom and justice for our fellow man on every continent.' "*

Exactly one year later, the nation's new 50-star flag was unfurled over Fort McHenry for its first official appearance anywhere in the world. As he had done in 1959, Secretary Seaton hoisted the latest edition of the Star-Spangled Banner into place.

A red rocket arching high over the ramparts of the fort signaled the start of the raising. An estimated 40,000 people watched from the field south of the fort as the flag inched its way skyward in the glare of five spotlights. As the "broad stripes and bright stars" rose, the huge throng broke into "The Star-Spangled Banner." As the last note of the anthem sounded, a battery of howitzers on the Patapsco River shore boomed a 50-gun salute. The fiftieth shell casing was sent to Governor William F. Quinn, of Hawaii, in commemoration of the event.

The 50-star flag was hailed most proudly by a delegation of 100 Hawaiians, whose florid "aloha shirts" and full length muumuus shone against the more somber Maryland hues. Leading the delegation was Representative Daniel K. Inouye, who took office when Hawaii was admitted to the Union on August 21, 1960.

At just about the time the flag pole brace was unearthed, two other discoveries were made. One was the boundary wall constructed in 1816–1817; the other was the site of the tavern which was an integral part of life at the fort during the early 19th century.

Archaeologists and historians have determined that in 1814 a wooden rail fence was constructed to separate public property from government land and to keep the animals of nearby farmers from intruding. By 1816, fort officials decided that a more permanent barrier was necessary, and work was begun on a brick wall about one and a half bricks thick and possibly ten feet high. Historians discovered that the wall appeared on the Plan of Fort McHenry by W. T. Poussin of 1819 and again on plans drawn in 1834. The wall was torn down in 1837 when additional land surrounding the fort was purchased.

The matter of the tavern is a longer story.

On November 6, 1798, one Philip Schwartzour purchased five and three-quarters acres adjacent to Fort McHenry from William Goodwin for $2,000. On the property at that time were a two-story brick building with two rooms on each floor, a detached kitchen, and a small frame building with one room each on the first and second floors.

Displaying what must be acknowledged as a sharp business sense, Schwartzour transformed the complex into a tavern. The place immediately became a thorn in the side of the authorities at Fort McHenry, something it was to remain for the next 38 years. Even so, much of the color and vitality of life at Fort McHenry came to be associated with it. So, too, did some of the violence.

The opening of the tavern came just in time to take advantage of this nation's greatest alcoholic binge. Americans had been hard drinkers throughout their colonial past, but between 1800 and 1830, perhaps because of the expanded production of whiskies and the social disruption spawned by rapid growth and institutional change, citizens of the new republic drank more than ever before.

Despite the altercations that plagued Schwartzour's tavern, records show that the Army began to rent rooms there almost from the day of its opening. In the fall of 1799, Jean Foncin, the French engineer, stayed there while redesigning the fort. Lieutenant James House, paymaster for the 1st Regiment, rented a room at the tavern from December 10, 1799, to March 10, 1800, for the sum of $36.00.

The day after the bombardment, Captain Daniel Schwartzour, son of the owner, held a celebration at his family's establishment. It lasted three days and became an annual event well attended every year.

In January, 1818, General Joseph G. Swift, Chief of Engineers, wrote the following letter to John C. Calhoun, Secretary of War:

> *"I enclose a copy of a letter and a sketch received from Colonel George Armistead who commands Fort McHenry near Baltimore. I had required Colonel Armistead to ascertain the piece of land adjacent to the Fort McHenry which land should, in my opinion, belong to the United States for the purpose of allowing expansion of the existing defenses and to keep tavern keeping and the troublesome neighbors from the immediate vicinity of the Fort. A large brick tavern now standing contingent to the Fort, has for many years been a troublesome place. This building should be taken down not only for the reason just mentioned, but also to prevent its being used as a cover to an enemy in case of any future attack upon the Fort."*

Notwithstanding the urgency of this letter, the War Department delayed any action in securing the property until 18 years later.

On April 4, 1833, the commandant of Fort McHenry, Colonel J. B. Walbach, wrote General N. S. Jesup, Quartermaster U.S. Army, about the possibility of renting the rooms above the tavern for the new doctor and two of his assistants. He said: "The only difficulty with regard to renting was the uncertainty of the time of the lease, yet to have such neighbors [the tavern] in our vicinity, and in fact adjoining the walls of the Post, is a great nuisance, and as our present soldiers are generally addicted to intemperance, it is impossible to prevent the introduction, or rather smuggling in of that infernal bane for our Army: WHISKEY."

Again on June 27, 1833, the commandant wrote General Jesup a letter which said in part:

"Between the alternative of leasing the 5¾ lot for ten years and repairing the building at the public's expense, or purchasing the property at $12,000. I should choose the latter, notwithstanding—I think the price unreasonable. I should do so, not because it is a better bargain for the present, but because it will be so in the end. Situated as it is at the main entrance to the work, and being occupied as a tavern, it is a source of serious annoyance to the garrison, both from its character and its proximity."

Instead of buying, however, the government continued to lease part of the property for the next several years. Meanwhile, in 1811, Philip Schwartzour had died, leaving his wife to run the tavern until 1836, when, on January 4, she had a realtor place the following advertisement in the *Batlimore American:*

PUBLIC SALE

Fort McHenry property—*I shall sell at public sale on Thursday the 28th January, at 1 o'clock at the Exchange 5¾ acres of land more or less adjoining the Fort, and at present in the occupancy of the United States. The improvements on the land consist of an extensive and well built two story Brick Building, fronting on the road and adjoining the Fort wall, about 50 feet, and running back 150 feet more or less. This building has a hall, parlour, and a number of convenient chambers, with an extensive back building, and has heretofore been occupied as a tavern. Also directly opposite the above is a frame building, about 25 feet front running back 50 feet. This property has a waterfront of 500 feet. Possession will be given to the purchaser on the 1st of February, 1836, at which time the part leased to the United States expires. Terms of sale ½ cash, 6 months, and ½, 9 months for approved note with security, bearing interest from day of sale."*

J. I. Gross, Realtor

Immediately the commandant of Fort McHenry sent a copy of the advertisement

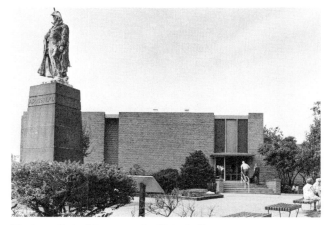

Sharing a Quiet Moment at the Visitor's Center

Sydney S. Sussman

Ranger Paul Plamann interprets the fort's history for visitors   *Sydney S. Sussman*

to General Jesup with a notation that if the property were bought by an individual it would remain a great nuisance to his command. He further stated that it was his hope that it was not too late to have the amount required to purchase the property attained during the then-current session of Congress.

But, no doubt to the commandant's dismay, the sale was cancelled. One daughter, who opposed the transaction, had filed suit against her mother, brother, and sister. Finally, on September 26, 1836, the court appointed Richard W. Gill as trustee for the sale of the property at public auction.

The auction was held on November 15, 1836, and the successful bidder was General Charles Gratiot, Chief of Engineering U.S. Army, who purchased the property for $12,001. For the next seven years the Army used the buildings as *it* saw fit: to house the medical staff at the fort. But then, in 1843, because of the deterioration of the buildings and lack of funds for renovation, the Army demolished the entire complex.

Fortunately, remnants of it seem to have been found. Archaeologists have discovered the cellar of a building of the late 18th century filled with brick and plaster fragments and with kitchen and household debris. They also found a piece of a circa-1814 bombshell which was probably tossed there with other refuse. The floor of the cellar was native clay, and the walls may have been five to six feet in height. By consulting the plan of the fort in 1803, which showed the larger tavern building to be approximately 30 by 54 feet, the same size as the cellar, it was determined that this was indeed the site of the tavern building which had been operated by the Schwartzours.

Though the building has been destroyed, its memory cannot be. A tankard which the defenders used to toast their victory at the annual post-war celebrations still exists and is in the possession of the Maryland Historical Society.

Then, too, the tavern was the place—and the annual celebrations there were the occasions—from which the Society of the War of 1812 had its inception. It is the hope of the Society, the only national patriotic organization which Baltimore can claim as its own, that the tavern can some day be reconstructed as its headquarters.

One of the archaeologists' most recent finds was the foundation of a traverse—an extra interior wall designed to protect the defenders in the event of a "last stand." It was discovered by accident. In the fall of 1981, the National Park Service decided to replace a macadam walkway with a brick one. Since federal laws required park officials to be sure no historical memorabilia would be destroyed by the bricklayers, archaeologist William Stokinger began to dig around the macadam. There he discovered a granite slab which he theorized was the base of a traverse wall built to protect the main gate from exploding bombshells.

David Orr, Regional Archaeologist for the Mid-Atlantic Region of the National Park Service, was called in to verify this important discovery. The traverse wall foundation was the rock slab discovered inside the arched entrance of the fort. Orr said the traverse was six feet high, eight feet wide and 12 feet long. It was constructed of brick and earth.

A letter dated May 19, 1813, was found in the National Archives by Scott Sheads, Fort McHenry National Park Service Ranger-Historian, which confirmed the existence of the traverse at the time of the bombardment.

The letter states that Major Beall "had erected a traverse inside the fort in front of the gateway and one in front of the magazine" on orders from the War Department and Army Corps of Engineers.

This traverse joins quite a number of other major finds which have been made over the years at Fort McHenry—among them the 1813 shot furnace and well, and the ravelin bridge entrance. Many small artifacts have also been found, such as: three small cannons, two 18-pound cannon balls, one 10-pound cannon ball, uniform buttons, belt buckles, glasses, and pottery . . . each piece a minor actor in the unforgettable drama that was played at Fort McHenry through the years.

TATTOO CEREMONIES
AND "SPIRITS"

FORT MCHENRY TODAY is more than a military museum, more than a passive relic of the past. It is still a very active place—especially in the summer months, when many special events are held.

Perhaps the most dramatic of the events is the Tattoo Ceremony, which has been held since 1965 on Sunday evenings during the summer.

In the modern armed forces, Tattoo is simply a bugle call. It is sounded exactly 15 minutes prior to lights out in barracks and on ships of war. It is the longest and liveliest call of the day. It is a tradition.

In the early 18th century, however, when military signals were the prime concern of buglers and drummers, Tattoo was not just a tradition; it was a very practical signal. It began as "Tap Toe," "Tap" referring to the ale taps of the taverns, and "Toe" meaning to shut or close. Eventually, soldiers' slang slurred the term "Tap Toe" into "Tattoo." At a designated time, the field musics would march around to the local taverns, playing to signal the approach of Tattoo. As soon as the soldiers heard the call they would rush back to the fort. When the field musics completed their rounds, they too would return to the fort, where the sergeant major would command them to "Sound Tattoo."

Unlike standard parades, the formation itself followed no definite set of rules. Instead, each regiment developed its own ceremony. The Tattoo was a good gauge of a unit's personality. For some it was a simple muster; for others it became an almost theatrical performance, even featuring fireworks. The Tattoo was developed to suit its surroundings, but the basic elements remained the same: the muster, the publication of orders and instructions, an exercise of certain drills to prove the troops fit for their duties, a salute to the colonel, if that gentleman happened to look in on the formation, and finally a march in review.

The Fort McHenry Tattoo contains all of these elements, blending precision drills and exciting musical arrangements into a stirring military program for the whole family. In addition, a special tribute is paid to the Star-Spangled Banner which flies overhead. Featured in the display of military pageantry are units from the United States Air Force, Army, Coast Guard, Marine Corps, and Navy, each performing on different evenings. Since 1982, the Fort McHenry Guard has taken an active role in the Tattoo ceremonies.

The Guard was organized in the fall of 1981. It is composed of volunteers-in-

parks who are dedicated to the preservation of the history of the troops who served at Fort McHenry when it was an active military post. Although the current program deals with the men who were stationed there during the War of 1812, the Guard is also interested in the personnel who served at the fort during the Civil War, when it was used as a prison camp, and those who were there during World War I, when the hospital was operating on the grounds. The volunteers who make up The Fort McHenry Guard are drawn from a variety of occupations and backgrounds, but they all share a common interest in the history of the fort.

Although the Guard officially took the field for the first time in the summer of 1982, its creation was the culmination of years of research on the uniforms, weapons, and equipment used during the War of 1812. In addition, extensive research was conducted on the city of Baltimore to enable the guard to portray an accurate picture of life at the fort in 1814 as the city prepared for the expected British attack.

In that summer of 1814, there were four major military groups at Fort McHenry, and the Guard recreates examples of three. The regular garrison consisted of the 3rd Regiment of Artillery from the United States Army. Members of the Guard who represent that regiment wear a distinctive uniform highlighted by a dark blue wool coat with red facings and yellow trim. Their round felt hats are topped with a red plume. Each soldier wears a white belt over each shoulder to carry a cartridge box and a bayonet and is also armed with a smooth-bore musket. Even though these men were part of the artillery, they were expected to be able to defend their cannon from the enemy.

The second group represented by the Guard are members of the Maryland militia who were ordered into Fort McHenry to reinforce the regular garrison. During the summer of 1814, these men, many of whom were wealthy merchants from Baltimore, came into the fort for a week at a time to drill with musket and cannon. The militiamen wear a uniform that reflects stylistic trends of the time. Their long blue coats with red facings give these men a gentlemanly look which reflects their upper-class background. Their half-moon hats are more fashionable than functional, as members of the Guard will attest.

The final group represented by the Fort McHenry Guard are the U.S. Sea Fencibles. These men represented the maritime community of Baltimore. Many had served aboard the privateers that ravaged British shipping in the early days of the War of 1812. In 1814, they rallied to defend the city by fighting on land. These lads of the ocean on shore dressed in plainer seamen's attire. Nonetheless, they drilled long hours so they would be proficient fighters when the British attack came.

The Fort McHenry Guard does not portray the U.S. Marine Corps because—from the halls of Montezuma to the shores of Baltimore—the U.S. Marine Corps represents itself on ceremonial occasions.

The programs presented by the Guard are made even more interesting by the fact that the men are living and acting as 1814 soldiers. All members of the Guard are well versed in both the history of the fort and the everyday life of the soldiers who were stationed there, and they are willing to answer any questions that visitors may have.

In 1972, a portion of the seawall was damaged when hurricane "Agnes" struck Baltimore. The National Park Service, in the fall of 1974, launched a project to repair the seawall. Some of the 1,200 foot wall was rebuilt, but only after huge boulders extending some 600 feet into the water had been piled in front of it to lessen the pressure upon it. Extensive repairs were made on the bomb shelters, walks, and brick and stonework of the star fort.

Tattoo Ceremony, 1960's
A. Aubrey Bodine

August 1983 Tattoo Ceremony—Fort McHenry Guard (foreground), U.S. Army's Old Guard (background) *Bob Willis*

In the pre-dawn of July 4, 1975, some 70,000 early risers witnessed the start of the Bicentennial celebration "By Dawn's Early Light," a reenactment of the 1814 British bombardment. Afterwards, there was a dramatic presentation portraying the writing of the national anthem by Francis Scott Key. It in turn was followed by an interfaith service led by Lawrence Cardinal Shehan, retired Baltimore archbishop.

At 8 P.M. President Gerald R. Ford and Mrs. Ford arrived at Fort McHenry by helicopter. After their arrival, President and Mrs. Ford watched 41 immigrants from 15 countries take their oath as new citizens of the United States. "We are honored," the President said, "that they have chosen what we often take for granted."

President Ford then delivered a patriotic message about his hopes for the future of America. "Our third century, I believe should be an era of individual freedom," President Ford told the flag-waving crowd. "A mass approach of a modern world places a premium on creativity and individuality. This is a celebration of liberty, freedom and democracy wherever they exist and America today is a strong and great nation. It still lives the values of its Declaration, its Constitution, its Bill of Rights. It still remains— in Lincoln's words—the last hope of earth," the President said.

At the suggestion of park technician John Daley, the National Park Service staff had taken up a collection to purchase and present to President Ford the 15-star flag which was flown over the fort in his honor.

"I was a park ranger myself," the President responded, "a 90-day wonder, and I appreciate the job you're doing."

Mr. Daley rejoined, "Mr. President, you've come a long way!"

Since 1978 there have been Civil War Weekends at the fort in the fall and spring. These depict the living conditions and the events which took place in the fort during the Civil War period. Participants live at the fort each weekend.

But the recreators of 1812 and Civil War troops are not the only "spirits of the past" at Fort Mchenry. There is, for instance, the spectral Levi Claggett.

As we have noted, during the September 13th attack on the fort, a British bomb scored a direct hit on a gun position. Lieutenant Claggett was killed—or so it was recorded. Some people think he lives on at the fort . . . they think, that is, that his *spirit* lives on.

There are those who insist they have seen him—or felt his presence—there. A park ranger reported that one cold and rainy day, he performed his usual tour duty of the star fort. The fort was practically deserted due to the bad weather. As he exited one of the buildings, however, he saw the shadow of a man on a wall. Moving closer to it, he determined that it was not his own shadow. On inspection of the surrounding buildings, he could find no other visitors. Although he mentioned it to no one at the fort, another ranger had a similar experience later in the day, but also heard footsteps. Again, the fort was deserted. Later, when the rangers compared notes, they discovered that the shadow and the footsteps occurred in front of the building that overlooked the spot where Claggett was killed.

But Claggett may not be the only shade haunting the historic bastions, for there is the mysterious matter of Private John Drew.

Drew, a 28 year-old native of Richmond, Virginia, had stood guard duty on the outer battery during the night of November 14, 1880. The next morning, when his relief arrived, he was found asleep. Placed under arrest, Drew was taken to the guardhouse and told by a sergeant to clean out his cell before being locked in. Drew obliged, but, in the process, he picked up a rifle leaning against the wall and slipped it into his cell. Later, when he was alone, he stuck the muzzle into his mouth and pulled the trigger with his toe.

Some speculate that because Drew shirked his responsibility in life, he has been condemned to stand eternal guard duty at Fort McHenry. Indeed, if one small dog belonging to a Park Service ranger could talk, he might give some validity to this story. One evening the dog, out for his tour of the seawall, came upon the exact spot near the outer battery where Private Drew had been discovered sleeping on the job. The dog apparently sensed the presence of someone walking toward him—he growled and cowered, then hurried back to the safety of his owner. Together, they headed back to the fort itself.

Coincidence, hoax, or just plain power of suggestion? There will always be two kinds of people: those who believe in ghosts and those who don't. At Fort McHenry, it's doubtful that the spirits question their own existence. They surely must know whether they're here or . . . there.

On August 7, 1983, the National Park Service celebrated its 50th year at Fort McHenry with a special sunset Tattoo Ceremony. After performances by the U.S. Army "Old Guard" Fife and Drum Corps and the Color Guard and Drill Team from Fort Myer, Virginia, the Fort McHenry Guard sounded taps as the Star-Spangled Banner waved in the evening breezes from the Patapsco.

Baltimore's Mayor, William Donald Schaefer, spoke of the importance of the fort to the City of Baltimore. He said that to stand within the star fort was "like being a part of the history that was created here, at this very spot." Paying tribute to the brave soldiers and citizens of the city who made their stand for freedom at Fort McHenry on a September night in 1814, he said that "the course of history was, indeed, changed by the actions of these courageous men" who "provided an inspiration to all men who love liberty."

The Mayor congratulated the Park Service on maintaining and preserving "this shrine of great deeds, valor and resolution" and said that it was important for our future generations that this fort be preserved so that lessons won here by brave men will never be forgotten.

Calling Fort McHenry, "our friend here by the entrance to the harbor," he said that if one ever needed to be reminded of "this country's greatness, they can look over to Fort McHenry and see Freedom, the flag waving 24 hours a day over this great and historic fort."

Mayor William Donald Schaefer, at the 50th Anniversary of the fort as a National Park.   *National Park Service*

EPILOGUE

FORT MCHENRY was a bastion of tyranny during the Civil War, a place of hope and healing during World War I.

But the singularity of Fort McHenry's place in American history derives exclusively from the fortuitous concurrance of circumstances during a mere 25 hours in 1814. We have seen what those circumstances were: a triumphant military victory over an invading enemy . . . the flying of a great flag to symbolize a city's—a nation's—determination to remain free . . . the presence of a poet who was inspired to sing of what he saw.

To visit Fort McHenry today, to stand upon its ramparts and watch the Stars and Stripes wave high overhead, is to sense across the years those few proud hours when *"The Star-Spangled Banner"*—our country's stirring national anthem—was born.

> *Romantic Lyre was never thrilled,*
> *Nor Homer's harp aspiring rung,*
> *By deed heroic nobler than*
> *Those of our own land yet unsung,*
> *Then join the anthem of the brave;*
> *Sing of Patapsco's shining wave,*
> *That gave to Freedom's golden age*
> *The thrice illustrious heritage*
> *Of gallant Fort McHenry!*
>
> *John F. Gontrum*

REFERENCE NOTES

Prologue
Poems of Fort McHenry, John Gontrum

The Building Years—1661–1811
1974 Historic Structure Report—Fort McHenry, Historical and Architectural Data, Erwin N. Thompson and Robert D. Newcomb—Historical and Archaeological Research Project Library, Fort McHenry*
Records of the Maryland Council of Safety, File Book 1780 HARP
Correspondence of James McHenry, File Book 1800 HARP
1607–1896, Who Was Who In America, Edited by A.N. Marquis Co.
Maryland's Religious History, Maryland Historical Society Magazine, Volume 21

The War Clouds Gather
Fort McHenry National Monument & Historic Shrine, Harold I. Lessem and George C. Mackenzie HARP
Dawn's Early Light, Walter Lord
File Book 1813 HARP
File Book 1814 HARP

The Enemy is Upon Us!
Dawn's Early Light, Lord
Fort McHenry National Monument & Historic Shrine, Lessem & Mackenzie
File Book 1813 HARP
File Book 1814 HARP

The Bombardment
Dawn's Early Light, Lord
Old Baltimore, Annie Leakin Souissant
File Book 1814 HARP
File Book 1815 HARP
Pictorial Fieldbook of the War of 1812, Benson Lossing
Fort McHenry National Monument & Historic Shrine, Lessem & Mackenzie

The Star-Spangled Banner—The Poem and the Flag
Star-Spangled Banner—Centennial Publication, 1914, Baltimore City, Mayor and City Council
Fort McHenry National Monument & Historic Shrine, Lessem & Mackenzie
Dawn's Early Light, Lord
Early American Life, October 1983

The Aftermath—Honor and Peace
Dawn's Early Light, Lord
Baltimore Patriot, April 27, 1818
Chruch Records of St. Paul's Church and Cemetery, Maryland Historical Society
American Daily & Commercial Advertiser, October 9, 1824
Travels Through North America During the Years 1825 and 1826, Karl Bernhard, The Duke of Saxe-Weimar Eisenbach
Niles National Register, April 27, 1839

Civil War Years
Baltimore and the 19th of April, 1816, George William Brown
Memoirs of John Adams Dix, Edited by Morgan Dix
Diary of Benjamin Gunter HARP
American Bastille, John A. Marshall
Diary of Henry Hall Brogden HARP
Diary of George Washington Kimball HARP
Marshall & Taney, Statesmen of the Law, Ben W. Palmer
The Milligan Case, Edited by Samuel Klaus
Without Fear or Favor, A Biography of Chief Justice Roger Brooke Taney, Walker Lewis

A Pause and The Centennial
File Book 1879 HARP
File Book 1883 HARP
Baltimore Sunpapers
Baltimore News American

World War I—The Hospital
The Troublebuster, U.S. General Hospital No. 2 Fort McHenry HARP
Diary of Emily Raine Williams, U.S. General Hospital No. 2, Fort McHenry HARP
File Books 1916–1922 HARP

Fort McHenry, A National Park
Baltimore Sunpapers
File Books 1922–1935 HARP

Historic Raisings and the Tavern
1974 Historic Structure Report—Fort McHenry, Historical and Architectural Data, Thompson and Newcomb
Archaeological Investigations of Fort McHenry National Monument and Historic Shrine (1981), Bryan L. Avazian, William Stokinger, Patricia E. Rubertone, and Lawrence E. Babits
File Books 1798–1850 HARP
Legal Papers of Philip Schwartzour, Maryland Hall of Records

Epilogue
Poems of Fort McHenry, John Gontrum

hereinafter referred to as "HARP"

BIBLIOGRAPHY AND CREDITS

Dawn's Early Light, Walter Lord, *W. W. Norton & Co., Inc., NY 1972*

Old Baltimore, Annie Leakin Sioussant, *The McMillan Co. NY 1931*

Without Fear or Favor, A Biography of Chief Justice Roger Brooke Taney, Walker Lewis, *Houghton, Mifflin Company, Boston 1965*

Marshall & Taney, Statesmen of the Law, Ben W. Palmer, *Russell & Russell, NY 1966*

The Milligan Case, Edited by Samuel Klaus, *Alfred A. Knopf, NY 1929*

National Star-Spangled Banner Centennial, Official Programme & The Story of Baltimore, *National Star-Spangled Banner Centennial Commission 1914, Mayor and City Council of Baltimore*

Poems of Fort McHenry, John Gontrum, *Lord Baltimore Press, Baltimore, 1911*

Historic Structure Report, Fort McHenry, Erwin N. Thompson & Robert D. Newcomb, *National Park Service, Denver 1974*

Archaeological Investigations of Fort McHenry National Monument and Historic Shrine, Bryan L. Avazian, William Stokinger, Patricia Rubertone, Lawrence E. Babits, *National Park Service, Denver, 1981*

American Bastille, John A. Marshall, *T. Hurley, Philadelphia, 1870*

Baltimore & the 19th of April 1861, George William Brown, *Maclay & Associates, Baltimore, 1982*

Travels Through North America During the Years 1825 and 1826, Karl Bernhard, The Duke of Saxe-Weimar Eisenach *Carey, Lea & Carey, Philadelphia 1828*

Pictorial Fieldbook of the War of 1812, Benson Lossing, *Harper & Bros., New York, 1869*

Memoirs of John Adams Dix, Edited by Morgan Dix, *Harper & Bros., New York 1883*

1607–1896, Who Was Who In America, *A. N. Marquis Company, Chicago, 1967*

CREDITS

Produced by Stanley L. Cahn
Designed by Mossman Art Studio
Military Uniforms and Accouterments—
research by John H. McGarry, III
and artwork by Stanley Mossman
Typography by Monotype Composition Co.
Printed by Port City Press, Inc.
on Warren's Patina

ILLUSTRATIONS

ILLUSTRATIONS

INDEX

INDEX

ABOUT THE AUTHOR

Norman G. Rukert was born in Baltimore in 1915. After graduating from City College at the age of 15, he entered his father's waterfront terminal business. Over the past half century his career has ranged from pier laborer to chairman of the board of Rukert Terminals Corporation, a position he attained in February 1980 after serving as president for 19 years.

He has long had an interest in historical data and restoration. Under his direction, the Rukert-owned Brown's Wharf, Baltimore's oldest warehouse, was renovated and established as a maritime museum in Fells Point. For this achievement, he received the Mayor's Award in 1977 and the Baltimore Heritage Award in 1979. He has recently restored a building that is an authentic late 18th century merchant's home, with the first floor serving as an exhibit hall and reception center for the maritime museum on Thames Street.

Mr. Rukert was named Man of the Year by the Junior Chamber of Commerce in 1976, and in 1977 he was honored with the Bell Award for Outstanding Contribution to the maritime industry. In 1979, he received the first William Fell Public Service Award for leadership in port related industry and exemplary public service. In 1983 the Traffic Club of Baltimore named him Man of the Year for outstanding contributions to the transportation industry.

He serves as Chairman of the Radcliffe Maritime Museum of the Maryland Historical Society and is a member of three pivotal port-oriented committees of the Greater Baltimore Committee.

As an author, Mr. Rukert has contributed four successful maritime histories: "Fells Point Story" (1976) "Historic Canton" (1978) "Federal Hill" (1980) "The Port, Pride of Baltimore" (1982) as well as the latest, "Fort McHenry, Home of the Brave". He has lectured widely on the subject.

He is married and has two children and four grandchildren.